Praise for

# I Sold My Soul on eBay

"What will strike you in the pages of this book is that Hemant isn't angry or antagonistic. As you try to figure out what exactly his agenda is, you'll probably arrive at the same conclusion I did. I think he's simply after the truth."

—ROB BELL, teaching pastor at Mars Hill Bible Church and author
of *Velvet Elvis* and *Sex God*

"Hemant Mehta, the self-proclaimed friendly atheist, gives us a third-eye view of how evangelical churches appear to the unchurched. I found myself intrigued and sometimes amused as he explained why churches keep atheists out instead of bringing them in. (By the way, you don't have to agree with everything Hemant says. He certainly doesn't agree with everything you and I say.)"

—RANDY FRAZEE, teaching pastor at Willow Creek Community Church
and author of *The Connecting Church* and *Making Room for Life*

"Sometimes the emperor just forgets to put on his shirt. But let's admit it: sometimes he really *is* naked. Hemant is the honest voice at the side of the parade, giving us a rare take on how our weekly gatherings really come off to nonbelievers. It's hilarious. It's excruciating. But most of all, it's honest. That alone makes this book a keeper."

—SALLY MORGENTHALER, author, and founder of Worship Evangelism
(www.trueconversations.com)

"If you work in a church, attend a church, or are interested in how a person without religion thinks, you'll want to read this book."

—MARK PAROLINI, in *Aspiring Retail*

"When a normal, nonbelieving guy like Hemant offers to honestly evaluate Christians as we work with those who don't think like we do, we should take notice. This book helps Christians find ways to better attract and love the growing number of people who aren't buying the Christian party line…but who are honestly searching for answers."

—DR. TIM HARLOW, senior pastor of Parkview Christian Church
in Orland Park, Illinois

"I winced, I laughed, and I learned as I read Hemant's descriptions of his visits to churches around the country. This book is a gift to all of us who seek to reach and engage those beyond our four walls. It changed the way I preached yesterday, and I suspect there will be more changes as I work out the implications for our church."

—REV. LAURA TRUAX, senior pastor of LaSalle Street Church in Chicago

"As I read Hemant's observations about the good, the bad, and the ugly of church, I couldn't help but notice how often I agreed with him. I was stunned to find an atheist who seems to understand the inclusive, life-changing, and world-serving mission of the church better than some Christians do. Read this book with an open mind and a willingness to learn from someone you might disagree with, but who will gain your respect."

—MIKE CLAWSON, pastor of Via Christus Community Church and coordinator of up/rooted, the Chicagoland Emergent Cohort

"Mirrors are helpful in two ways: they can help us see things about ourselves that we need to change, or they can confirm that things are just as we intend them to be. In this book, Hemant holds up a mirror to American churches. Don't blame the mirror if you're surprised by what you see."

—BRUXY CAVEY, teaching pastor at The Meeting House in the Toronto area (www.themeetinghouse.ca)

"I was lucky enough to buy Hemant's soul on eBay, and we became good friends. I asked him to review ten churches and record his impressions on his blog. Thousands of people read his insightful critiques, and hundreds posted comments. I'm convinced that what Hemant has to say is critical to Christians who want to connect with the people Jesus misses most."

—JIM HENDERSON, executive director of Off the Map (www.off-the-map.org) and author of *Evangelism Without Additives* and *Jim and Casper Go to Church*

# I Sold My Soul on eBay

## Viewing Faith Through an Atheist's Eyes

# Hemant Mehta

Foreword by Rob Bell, best-selling author of *Velvet Elvis*

WATERBROOK
PRESS

I Sold My Soul on eBay
Published by WaterBrook Press
12265 Oracle Boulevard, Suite 200
Colorado Springs, Colorado 80921
*A division of Random House Inc.*

Italics in Scripture quotations reflect the author's added emphasis.

ISBN 978-1-4000-7347-4

Library of Congress Cataloging-in-Publication Data
Mehta, Hemant.
    I sold my soul on eBay : viewing faith through an atheist's eyes / Hemant Mehta. — 1st ed.
        p. cm.
Includes bibliographical references.
    ISBN 978-1-4000-7347-4
    1. Church.  2. Evangelistic work.  3. Non-church-affiliated people.  4. Mehta, Hemant—Religion.  5. Atheists.  I. Title.
    BV640.M44 2007
    261.2'1—dc22

                                                                                2006038746

Printed in the United States of America
2007—First Edition

10 9 8 7 6 5 4 3 2 1

Special Sales

Most WaterBrook books are available in special quantity discounts when purchased in bulk by corporations, organizations, and special interest groups. Custom imprinting or excerpting can also be done to fit special needs. For information, please e-mail Special Markets@WaterBrookPress.com or call 1-800-603-7051.

*For Mom, Dad, and Nina.*

# Contents

# Publisher's Note

If you were looking for God, where would you go to find Him? Better yet, if you had decided God doesn't exist, what would you do to test that conclusion?

For author Hemant Mehta, a leader in the Secular Student Alliance and other secular organizations, the God question is a crucial one. He would be the first to acknowledge that many questions are left unanswered. And while he trusts science to prove or disprove most theories and assumptions, he agrees that the question of God is not one science can be expected to answer.

So in answer to the question, "If you were looking for God, where would you go to find Him?" Mehta decided to give church a try. But he didn't decide *just* to go to church. He held an eBay auction, agreeing to attend any place (or places) of worship determined by the winning bidder. Jim Henderson, a former pastor and author of *Evangelism Without Additives,* won the auction. He asked Mehta to attend a number of churches and write a critique of each one. The critiques were posted on Henderson's Web site, www.off-the-map.org, and readers were given a rare opportunity to look at faith through the eyes of an atheist.

Many who were aware of Mehta's eBay auction felt it made about as much sense as Davy Crockett giving Santa Anna advice on the most effective way to lay siege to the Alamo. Or Peyton Manning shouting the particulars of the Colts' next play to the Pittsburgh defense. Why would an atheist volunteer to point out what is working effectively in church on Sunday morning and what is failing when it comes to getting the gospel message across to skeptical listeners? When you read this book, you'll find out.

*I Sold My Soul on eBay* is a first. A committed skeptic teamed up with a publishing house that produces books for the Christian market with the purpose of providing candid, insightful, and fair-minded critiques of a wide variety of churches. As he did research for this book, Mehta visited fifteen churches in four states, including some of the best-known churches in the country. His critiques of these churches are presented here for the first time.

If you've never gone to church with an atheist, this is your chance to do so. We promise you'll be surprised, enlightened, amused, and sometimes unsettled by Mehta's assessment of what churches sound like, look like, and feel like to a curious outsider.

# FOREWORD

I knew I would love talking with Hemant Mehta long before I met him—I have much in common with atheists. What I find time and again is that the god they've rejected is a god I've rejected.

The god who doesn't encourage intellectual honesty, the god who doesn't care about the environment because "it's all going to burn," the god who calls the anemic words of bored worshipers going through the motions "praise," the god who would condemn billions of people to hell simply because they haven't said or done the proper ritual that Christians can't even agree on…

Some gods should be rejected.

And that, of course, is what makes Hemant's book so compelling. It's not just that he is smart, insightful, and honest. It's that so much of what he says is…well…true. What will strike you in the pages of this book is that Hemant isn't angry or antagonistic. As you try to figure out what exactly his agenda is, you'll probably arrive at the same conclusion I did.

I think he's simply after the truth.

After all, an atheist is a person of great conviction. It takes great faith to stare at a sunset, to hear a symphony in full swing, to watch a young child take her first steps, and not see something divine. And yet Hemant has his reasons…

Central to the life of a Christian is embracing the truth wherever you find it, living with the awareness that God can speak at any time, anywhere, through anyone.

This puts our friend Hemant in an unusual position: Lots of people in lots of churches will find this book very helpful in their efforts to put a face on God for the world we live in. So Hemant's work as an atheist will ultimately inspire people to live better lives in harmony with a God he doesn't believe in. It's beautiful, really.

As I sat with Hemant, talking about church and Jesus and faith and God, I couldn't help but think that his words and his search and his observations are going to be used in a powerful way to purify, convict, and spur the church of Jesus to be everything Jesus had in mind.

Because prophets can come from the most unexpected places, can't they?

—Rob Bell, teaching pastor at Mars Hill Bible Church
and author of *Velvet Elvis* and *Sex God*

# The Question of Faith

There once was a town that was the envy of all who lived outside it. The people in the town were happy, their businesses did well, and everyone was in good health. New residents arrived constantly, knowing they would be building their lives in a wonderful place. God was watching over the town.

One summer, however, things changed. Monsoons drenched the area, and most of the crops were washed away. Animals couldn't find shelter from the continual rain, and they were dying along with the crops. The people became depressed as they lost their sources of food and income—and watched their family members fall ill. The times were so bad that an atheist in the town went out one night and painted his credo on the side of a prominent building:

## GOD IS NOWHERE

When the townspeople saw this, they wanted more than anything for the man to be proven wrong. But they struggled to mount a convincing counter-argument. They had no reason to think God was still with them. If He were, wouldn't the rain let up? They went on with their business, wading always through inches of water, thinking no one could help them.

One day a wise monk visited the despondent community. He knew how beautiful the town had been, and he wondered what could have happened to destroy everyone's faith. He wanted to do something to restore the people's hopeful outlook on life.

As the monk walked through the town, observing the devastation, he realized the difficulty of his task. He stopped townspeople and asked what they were thinking. They told him God had left their village, and there was no one who could help them. They had no choice but to succumb to the misery. The monk assured them their lives would get better, but his words were easy to dismiss.

Then the monk rounded a corner and saw the atheist's message painted on the side of the building. Suddenly, he saw what had to be done.

The next day, as the townspeople passed the building, they saw a slightly altered message. Only one diagonal line had been added, and yet it changed everything. The message now read:

### GOD IS NOW/HERE

The change in the town was dramatic and immediate. When the people realized God was still with them, they became optimistic again. Maybe God had just been testing them, and for a while they may have failed the test. But now they knew they could withstand anything with God's help. The people realized their future was being looked after and their prayers would be answered. In no time at all, the town became prosperous again and the residents spread the word of God to every newcomer.[1]

This story served as my introduction to the world of other religions. At the age of five, I knew very little about religion or God. But I did know one thing: anyone who believed in a faith different from that of my family was wrong. I don't remember being taught that, I just picked it up indirectly from my parents and other adults who shared our religious beliefs. When my mom told me the story of the once-prosperous village, I don't think she intended to criticize other belief systems. She just wanted me to understand that God was great and if I said my prayers, according to our religious beliefs, I would be in His good graces.

I could understand the wonderful, sanguine message that the power and reach of God were incredible. But recalling the story now, almost twenty years later, I can't help but ask a number of questions: Where was this town? Why didn't they arrest the guy who vandalized the building? Wouldn't the monsoon rain wash away the freshly applied paint? And are you telling me that just one slash mark really changed everyone's thinking?

Such is the nature of a skeptical person. We don't put our confidence in fables that are meant only to inspire us. However, when my mom first told me that story, I thought it was true. She didn't issue a disclaimer that identified the story as fiction. Only after I began asking questions did the story begin to lose its credibility. And as I grew up, I heard other parables like this one from other religions, stories meant to teach moral lessons. While I understood them to be just lively fairy tales, I found that even adults believed them to be literally true, without bothering to raise the types of questions I had. *Why are people unwilling to examine and question their beliefs?* I wondered.

But such questions reflect who I am today, not me as a child. When I heard of the attitude change brought about by a simple punctuation mark, I welcomed the wisdom God brought, and I hoped I would be as blessed as the townspeople were whenever I went through a rough period. How horrible it must be to think God isn't around! If only the people had held on to their faith from the start, they would've been able to make it through the time of despair much more easily. And I was saddened to learn that whoever these atheists were, they didn't believe in God.

I guess the story produced its intended effect, since these thoughts stayed with me for years. Amazingly, even though my parents raised me in the Jain faith, I didn't recall my mom mentioning our religion in the story. As I talked more with people who were religious, I discovered that many of them had heard similar stories about atheists. In fact, many of the stories portrayed atheists in a more malicious light. It took another ten years, after I had become a teenager, before I realized the extent to which such prejudices and stereotypes colored the reputations of nonreligious people.

I have lived on both sides of the religion divide—first as a devout religious believer and, since age fourteen, as a person without religion. I am an atheist, but I don't fit the common stereotype held by so many in the religious community. I am not angry with God, and I don't want to rid the world of religion. In this book, as we talk about matters of belief and nonbelief, I hope you will think of me not simply as an atheist, but rather as a person with questions about faith, an openness to evidence that might contradict my current beliefs, and a curiosity about Christianity and its message. Please don't assume I am the enemy of religious belief. I'm not trying to tear down anyone's religion, and I don't pretend to have all the answers.

By way of introduction, my name is Hemant, and I'm a friendly atheist. I'm serious when I say that in this book I'm going to do my best to help improve the way churches present the Christian message.

I suspect a number of questions have popped into your mind already. *Is he so naive that he believes religious people care what people like him think about Christianity?* (I do think Christians care about how they present their message, and I would never consider that to be naiveté.) *Why isn't he capitalizing the words* atheist *and* atheism? (Because atheism is not a religion, and atheists do not adhere to any religion. So I don't capitalize the word as I would Methodist or Presbyterian.) *How is his name pronounced?* (I prefer HEH-mint.)

I agree that my assumption that committed Christians will listen to what a nonreligious person has to say about churches and the job they're doing is a bit of a stretch. No athlete ever risks asking the opposing team's captain for advice on running a particular play… Well, not unless there's a hidden agenda, right?

Honestly, I have no ulterior motive. In fact, coming from a religious background myself, one I will describe in chapter 2, I know how important a place of worship can be. The religious culture that centered on my Jain temple was a positive force in my life, and I always see how profoundly and positively religious belief affects the people I love. At the same time, I understand why so many people have chosen a life of nonbelief. I've been an active atheist for many years, and I chair the board of directors of a national secular organization. From your vantage point, I'm playing for the other team. I know exactly what the other side thinks and feels. And you'd be surprised how far off the mark many Christians' perceptions of atheists actually are.

## AT HOME WITH AN ATHEIST

I'm gazing at my bookshelf as I write this, and I'm convinced a stranger looking at my reading material wouldn't be able to determine my loyalties. There's a Bible that was given to me by a liberal high-school friend. There are enough pamphlets on Christianity, given to me during college, to last a lifetime. Lee Strobel's *The Case for Faith* sits next to Carl Sagan's *Cosmos,* while Tim LaHaye's *Mind Siege* finds a place next to Sam Harris's *The End of Faith.* There's a book by Norman Geisler and Frank Turek, educational material from

Americans United for Separation of Church and State, and a slew of magazines ranging from *Charisma* to *Maxim*. I mark my page in the Richard
Dawkins book I am currently reading with a bookmark that has the Beati-
tudes written on it. (The bookmark was sent to me by a woman who read
about my story in a newspaper.) Even my (religious, but not Christian) mom
is working her way through Joel Osteen's bestseller, *Your Best Life Now.* The
books aren't sitting on my shelf to confuse people. I actually read them and
enjoy them. And sometimes, dare I say it, I even disagree with what the scholars say.

But as I read Christian books, and as I spent months attending an amazing variety of churches in different parts of the country, I kept running across
a consistent and troubling truth about American Christianity. It is clear that
most churches have aligned themselves against nonreligious people. By
adopting this stance, Christians have turned off the people I would think they
want to connect with. The combative stance I've observed in many churches,
and from many Christians on an individual level, is an approach that causes
people to become apathetic—and even antagonistic—toward religion as a
whole. By displaying a negative attitude toward anyone outside the religious
community, people of faith make enemies of those who don't believe in the
same God they do.

My purpose in writing this book is not to convince you of the wrongness
of your belief and the rightness of mine. I don't expect to create any new atheists. But I do think religion/nonreligion is a significant issue that deserves our
careful attention. If people are turned off by the confrontational attitude
prevalent in many churches, they may be turned off to all religion. If this happens, atheism would be ignored as well. (This isn't to say atheism is a religion,
but it is a belief system, and like religion, it requires a large measure of intro-
spection.) Mounting controversy over religious differences could lead people
to simply ignore religion, which could prevent them from seeking the truth

that could lead to a fuller life. Apathy and indifference affect me—as a leader of an atheist group—as much as they affect you as a committed Christian.

## THE CHURCHGOING ATHEIST

In the past year, I've had a unique opportunity to visit a great number of church services, first as a result of my eBay auction and then as I did research for this book. I now have a strong sense of what works and what doesn't in terms of drawing people like me, young and spiritually curious, to a church. A Barna poll might indicate that youth and young adults are leaving churches in greater and greater numbers. But surveys tend not to go below the surface, and they don't provide practical solutions. I reside squarely in the demographic that churches want to reach. But based on what I have experienced, the things many churches are doing on Saturday night or Sunday morning are not the things that will pull in those who share my mind-set.

This book is unique in that I will share a perspective that many church leaders would never otherwise hear. If your church is interested in reaching out to non-Christians, you can discover workable solutions by listening closely to your target audience. I am a nonreligious young adult living in a major Midwestern city. I have many friends of various religious backgrounds, and I'm a leader among my secular peers. I am the type of person who would be an asset to your church.

I am not your enemy, and neither am I an apostate, since I never left Christianity. I don't haul around a load of antichurch baggage based on having suffered through a stifling, overly narrow church upbringing. Neither do I wrestle with bitterness over having been wronged by the church. My own religious upbringing differed sharply from the Christian faith. So I come to this churchgoing experiment with an open mind and a deep well of curiosity.

When I visit a church, I pay attention more carefully, I would think, than many who attend regularly. I can share honest opinions and fresh insights because all of this is largely new to me. Plus, I can express genuine feedback because I'm not a member of the church. Really, how many people would tell their own pastor that sitting through his sermons is akin to entering a thirty-minute coma?

In my initial church critiques, which were posted on a Christian Web site (www.off-the-map.org), I provided my candid reactions—both positive and negative—and the pastors listened. In many cases they appreciated my observations and suggestions. (I even received some thank-you e-mails.) Perhaps by considering a religious outsider's impressions—and let's face it, can you get any more extreme than an atheist?—pastors and other Christians can become more proficient at appealing to the people who have left the church with a similar disconnected feeling.

I'm aware of the good that churches can do. Churches can enrich people's lives in ways that everyone, including atheists, can support. Why would anyone oppose something that helps people live the best life possible?

You may wonder: *If he is serious about what he's saying, then why is he an atheist? Wouldn't it be disadvantageous to the atheist community if more people went to church?* Hardly. Yes, many church teachings conflict with atheists' beliefs, but no one can dispute a church's powerful potential to sustain a positive impact on a community. Atheists actually support many of the same values churches espouse. For example, we share the Christian ideal for people to live a moral, ethical life, even though we might have differences regarding where those boundaries are drawn. If people are going through problems, we also want to lift their spirits. And even though I'm an atheist, I believe churches accomplish this better than any other organization or institution.

In the chapters that follow, I will talk about how I transitioned from being a religious person to being an atheist and how my life has changed (both for better and for worse) as a result. If you know where my beliefs come from, you will better understand my church critiques that begin in chapter 5.

And I hope that as you read my story, you will discover that the common stereotypes about atheists and other nonreligious people are not as accurate as you might think. We are not anti-Christ, anti-God, communists, worshipers of Satan, or liberal Democrats (well, not all of us, anyway).

You will also hear what goes on in the mind of an atheist who is curious about Christianity as I attend a wide range of church services, from small-town parishes to megachurches with restaurants, bookstores, and escalators. I hope this book will encourage you to initiate discussions with the atheists and other nonreligious people you know—the ones who live in your neighborhood, repair your car, work at your company, attend class with you, and possibly even live in your home. It's not hard to find us. Talk to us (without preaching to us), have a conversation with us about a broad range of topics (religion doesn't dominate our thinking), and initiate a friendship. Don't go through life overlooking your neighbors and co-workers who are not religious. I've come across too many people who claim they've never met an atheist, much less spoken to one. I find that hard to believe, since the atheists I know come from all over the country and from all walks of life. It's time we started talking to one another.

When I started posting my church critiques on the Web, after I "sold my soul on eBay," an amazing thing happened. Christians and atheists started dialoging in response to my posts. People who previously might not have spoken with people from the other side of the religious divide started spirited, candid, respectful conversations. And these conversations went on and on. In fact, they continue to this day on my blog at www.friendlyatheist.com. The views of the people involved in the dialogue did not necessarily change, but they gained new understanding of various points of view. And they had a chance to make their beliefs clear to an audience that otherwise might not have been exposed to the reasons behind a person's faith commitment (or lack of faith). The conversation benefits everyone, believer and nonbeliever alike. I hope to enter into such a dialogue with you on my blog.

Before I take you to church with me, it's vital that you know where I'm coming from, as well as how the news stories about my eBay auction propelled me into the public eye. If you get to know me and understand what motivates me, you'll gain more benefit from my feedback on how Christians and churches are coming across to nonreligious people.

I hope you'll come away with the desire to talk to religious outsiders and learn where they really stand on the major questions dealing with faith. By dispelling the stereotypes we all have of those who believe differently than we do, we'll be able to focus our energies on much more positive goals. We can become friends rather than antagonists.

I write as a curious atheist, one who is willing to consider any compelling evidence for the existence of God. Before this book is finished, I will have attended some of the best-known churches in the country, and I will have listened to many stories about the power of God. I'm eager to hear your responses to my commentary as I take this journey.[2] And whether you are a believer or a person without religious belief, thank you for coming along with me.

# Selling My Soul on eBay

## How I Became a Churchgoing Atheist

You know your life has taken a strange turn when you go to teach at a high school where you have substituted only two times before, and when you introduce yourself as Mr. Mehta, the students respond, "Wait, aren't you the guy who sold his soul on eBay?"

Two thoughts immediately come to mind: *Well, I didn't actually sell my soul,* and, *This can't be good for my teaching career.*

The students must have either seen me on the evening news in Chicago or on the front page of the *Chicago Sun-Times.* I guess I had become something of a public figure, "the atheist who sold his soul on eBay." But I didn't initiate the Internet auction to generate publicity for myself. I don't mind being known as an atheist, but I don't aspire to poster-skeptic status.

In fact, I have never tried to sever all personal ties with religion. In the years following my de-conversion, I maintained ties to my religious community. I was raised in Jainism, and many of the immigrants with whom my Indian parents came to America shared the same faith. I may have left the God of my childhood, but my parents are still faithful Jains. Since becoming an atheist, I have noticed that as people grow older, they become much more reluctant to change. Atheists tend to remain atheists. The religious stay religious. Occasionally, eleventh-hour conversions occur, but overall it seems that people fail to question beliefs that have become safe and comfortable.

When you proclaim yourself an atheist at the age of fourteen, as I did, and remain an atheist with each passing year, you stop thinking about why you made this change in the first place. But at the age of twenty-two, while I was still confident in my nonbelief, I realized I had never been exposed to a Christian worship service...or a Muslim service...or any other non-Jain religious service for that matter. In the interest of seeing what else was out there, I felt compelled to attend religious services. I didn't want others to question the basis of my nonbelief: "You're an atheist only because you don't know what Christianity is all about!"

I admit I knew relatively little about the Christian faith outside what I had read or could gather through pop culture. However, I had read parts of the Bible and listened to a large number of televangelists as well as religious leaders when they were interviewed in the news. (When a good speaker is on television, it's hard for me to change the channel!) It's much easier to pick up information about Christianity in the news media than it is to learn about atheism that way, since atheism is so rarely talked about. It turned out I heard about atheists more often from Christian preachers on television than from any other source.

As I started paying closer attention to the views of high-profile Christians, I mentioned to some Christian friends that I was reading articles by Jerry Falwell and James Dobson, and my friends would cringe. I really did want to know what Christians were talking about, and I was learning that not all Christians agreed on which of their "representatives" I should be listening to.

My Christian friends insisted that the high-profile Christians most often quoted in the news were using religion to suit their own political agendas, and that most Christians were not as extreme when it came to issues such as gay rights and science education in public schools. They told me I should stop listening to the television preachers and start reading books such as *Mere Christianity* by C. S. Lewis. I didn't understand how it was possible to gain a misconception of the Christian faith by listening to Christian leaders, especially when these men were said to represent major segments of the church. More important, I rarely saw Christians use the media to point out that these men were wrong. I did realize, however, that the Christians I knew personally were less extreme in their political views.

If there was such a diversity of viewpoints among Christians, how would I find out what Christianity was really about? The Christians I spoke to told me if I really wanted to gain insight into Christianity, I would need to go to a church for myself. Well, I did want to learn more about Christian theology and why people believed it. I knew that if it made more sense than my secular views, I would have to alter my beliefs. So I decided the best thing to do was expose myself to church.

## THE DECISION TO "AUCTION OFF MY SOUL"

New Testament scholar (and atheist) Gerd Lüdemann delivered a speech at Middle Tennessee State University a few years ago. He lectured on the "hoax of the Resurrection." The vast majority of the student population strongly opposed his appearance on campus. Yet the students who ran the school newspaper defended the decision to invite Lüdemann to speak. The newspaper's editorial contended, "The reason we're [in college] is to immerse ourselves in original, new ideas and subject ourselves to diverse arguments. Every student should attend at least one lecture that differs from his or her current beliefs; if those beliefs can't stand under scrutiny, they aren't worth believing."[1] Although I agreed with that view, I had never followed the editorial's advice myself. Many other atheists had been raised as Christians, so they knew what they were leaving. But I lacked that experience.

I decided I would step inside a church. However, I knew this exploration would be pointless unless I could ask questions about the faith—the questions that had always troubled or confused me. Also, I wanted to document the journey so others could see what I was experiencing. If they were to comment on my experience, they needed to know what I was doing, so I had to find a way to publicize my idea. How do you manage to raise interest in a project that is so…unusual?

I thought about some of the stranger news stories I had read. There was the grilled-cheese sandwich with the image of the Virgin Mary on it, and the opportunity offered to temporarily tattoo a man's forehead with a company's logo.[2] Suddenly, I knew the answer: eBay! I would post my idea on the auction Web site and people could bid on where and how long I would attend church. Who cared about the money?—I just wanted people to understand what I was doing and what I hoped to accomplish.

At the time, I lived next to Old Saint Patrick's Church, a historical landmark that survived the Great Chicago Fire of 1871. Since Mass was held right next door, it seemed an ideal place to attend. However, I didn't want to limit myself to attending just that one church. I knew that even churches of the same denomination could vary dramatically depending on location and the demographics of the congregation. More people would be interested in this project if *they* could decide where I should go to church. Certainly, if I wanted to learn about Christianity, I should listen to the people who knew the nuances between the different denominations.

In fact, I decided to go even further. Did it have to be a Christian place of worship? Nope. I figured I'd keep my options as wide open as possible. Whoever won the auction could decide where I would attend religious services. I posted on www.ebay.com on a Friday night and labeled it: "Send an atheist to his local church!" I explained my proposal as follows:

I'm a 22-year-old atheist from Chicago. I stopped believing in God when I was 14. Currently, I am an active volunteer for a couple different national, secular organizations. For one of them, I am the editor of a newsletter that reaches over 1,000 atheist/agnostic college students. I have written several Letters to the Editor to newspapers in and around Chicago, espousing my atheistic beliefs when Church/State issues arose. My point being that I don't take my non-belief lightly. However, while I don't believe in God, I firmly believe I would immediately change those views if presented with evidence to the contrary. And at age 22, this is possibly the best chance anyone has of changing me.

So, here's my proposal. Every time I come home, I pass this old Irish church. I promise to go into that church every day—for a certain number of days—for at least an hour each visit. For every $10 you bid, I will go to the Church for 1 day. For $50, you would have me going to mass every day for a week.

My promise: I will go willingly and with an open mind. I will not say/do anything inappropriate. I will respectfully participate in service(s), speak to priests, volunteer with the church if possible, do my best to learn about the religious beliefs of the churchgoers, and make conversation with anyone who is willing to talk. (Though I do reserve the right to ask the person questions about the faith.)

I will record my visits through a journal, pictures, or whatever other method of proof you'd like—I will uphold my promise.

Will I become religious? Well, I don't know. I really do have an open mind, but no one has convinced me to change my mind so far. Then again, I have also never attended a real church service. Perhaps being around a group of people who will show me "the way" could do what no one else has done before.

If the Irish Church doesn't work for you, we'll just find some other place local to me. I'll go to any place of worship—a Christian Church, a Catholic Church *[revision: I realize a Catholic Church is a Christian Church...so let me rephrase. By Christian, I meant to differentiate Protestant from Catholic]*,[3] a Mosque, a Synagogue, etc. They're all nearby. Makes no difference to me, but perhaps it's your faith that could change the mind of this atheist.

I also assure you that if you bid on this, I will write an article about my experiences in the newsletter mentioned earlier. The article would reach over 1,000 college students who share my current views. Even if you don't end up changing my mind, perhaps you can change theirs.

If you have any questions about this auction, I'd be glad to answer them.

I initially considered attending religious services for just one dollar per worship service, since the church was right down the street from me. But I reconsidered that idea when I realized anyone with an allowance could have the power to plan my schedule for the next several Sundays. I also considered the time and expense involved in traveling to various locations, and I still needed to deal with my graduate-school workload, so one dollar might be too low. I started with a ten-dollar-a-day minimum, and I anticipated the winning bid to be just that—ten dollars. I even planned out my day: I would go to a church on a Sunday morning and then see a movie that afternoon. However, as the eBay ad described, I was willing to explore churches for more than just one Sunday.

I knew that many people who stumbled across the auction would wonder if this was some type of get-rich-quick scheme. Since the money wasn't the motivating factor, I later amended the auction, promising to donate the winning bid to a nonreligious group, the Secular Student Alliance. (I'm the chair of the SSA's board of directors.) I committed to this donation aspect so that if a rich religious person wanted to send me to church for life, at least that person would know the money was going to a secular organization.

To spread the message of my journey I sent e-mails to a few conservative bloggers, thinking they would get a kick out of this endeavor. I shared with them a little about who I was and what I was doing. I was willing to put myself out there if it meant people would hear about the concept and spread the word about what I was doing. In fact, several of them did blog about my efforts, and surprisingly, many painted it in a very positive light.

I also sent press releases to local newspapers. The *Chicago Tribune* didn't respond. Neither did the *Chicago Sun-Times.* But the *Daily Southtown,* perhaps upon learning that I had graduated from a local high school, called me and published a story a few days later—with the headline "Auction for Salvation"—on the front page.

Surprisingly, I received hardly any negative responses to my eBay post. I had assumed I would be receiving e-mails from religious people telling me hell had a spot reserved for me. But that wasn't the case at all. They were genuinely curious how this auction would impact my life and whether it would produce a change.

The onslaught of publicity led to well over ten thousand hits on the eBay Web site in less than a week. All of a sudden, my personal mission was the hot topic of blogs everywhere. E-mails regarding the "eBay Atheist" were being circulated almost virally. Midway through the auction, as the bidding approached a staggering one hundred dollars, interest in the project grew even higher.

Many potential bidders wrote to me to find out if I was serious about the possibility of going to a Christian church. From that, I gathered that it was mostly Christians who were entering bids. Other bids came from atheists who didn't want me to step foot in any church whatsoever—they told me they wanted to "save me" from the Christians. I hoped people from other faiths would join the auction, in an attempt to assure that I was exposed to their religion. But the responses seemed limited to Christians and atheists.

## AMBUSHED ON THE RADIO

During the week of the bidding, I received an e-mail from a radio program hosted by actor Kirk Cameron (remember the old television show *Growing Pains*?). His co-host, Todd Friel, invited me to be a guest on their show, and I gladly accepted. I knew how conservative Cameron was and how opposite our views were, but I was excited to have the chance to speak with him.

Once I picked up the phone to do the radio interview, I realized the eBay auction was not very high on their list of discussion topics. The interview barely touched on the auction, allowing only a couple of minutes for discussion. The remainder of the forty-minute segment consisted of Cameron and Friel preaching that God made the world and that my belief in the Big Bang was countered by the Great Big Cosmic 'Duh'—that God created the universe.[4]

I tried to explain that atheists rely on logic and reason, rather than faith, in all matters that can't be proven. Also, I pointed out that atheists don't automatically condemn those who think differently. We don't say, for instance, that nonatheists are eternally doomed because of what they believe. However, the radio-show hosts informed me over the airwaves that since I had not accepted Christ in my life, I was going to hell because I had committed sin. (I admitted in response to direct questions that I had lied before and had used God's name in vain as a figure of speech.)

I understand that Kirk Cameron needs to keep his radio show lively and interesting in order to attract listeners. But was insulting me really what it took to do that? Did all Christians feel that ridicule and condemnation were interesting and entertaining? I wasn't expecting Cameron to be a Christian

Howard Stern. Even beyond the question of attracting and entertaining listeners, are comments meant to embarrass a guest and a lack of kindness really accurate representations of Christian compassion? What happened to the lovable Mike Seaver I had seen Cameron portray years ago on *Growing Pains*?

I wondered if this was the sort of hostility I was about to step into for the next several weeks. What had I gotten myself into?

Even after I got off the line, the co-hosts of the radio show continued to emphasize what a fool I was for following atheism. Cameron was dissing me on national-broadcast and satellite radio. I could've gotten angry, but instead I was amused. Do you see the irony? Cameron's combative approach helped prove my point that the atheistic outlook is less antagonistic than the religious view.

The same week I did the radio interview, an e-mail arrived from a reporter named Suzanne. She was curious about why I was doing the eBay auction. We began exchanging e-mails about my reasons. And meanwhile, the auction was heating up.

## WHAT PRICE FOR AN ATHEIST'S SOUL?

During the course of the week, the eBay bids started escalating rapidly. The one-hundred-dollar bid quickly blossomed to three hundred. And there were still two days left!

On the last night, I sat at my computer, continually refreshing the screen to see if anything new had happened. While each click of the Refresh button did not reveal a higher bid, each click showed an increased number of people viewing the auction, meaning every few seconds a new rush of people had logged on to the page.

Anyone who has sold a product on eBay can tell you that the price of a popular item jumps dramatically in the last few seconds of an auction. Every bidder believes his or her bid will be the last one, but those who anticipate this onslaught bid higher than they normally would just to counter competing bidders. At this point, since the price was already at three hundred dollars, I didn't imagine it would go much higher.

With just under three minutes left, I realized I would be spending thirty hours—perhaps an hour every day for a month—at church. But before that idea settled in, another click of the Refresh button revealed the price to be over four hundred dollars. With only a few seconds left before the auction ended, the price shot up once again, this time to five hundred dollars! And before I could even process what just happened, the price spiked one last time to five hundred four dollars.

I was stunned. All I could think about was how the final bid was a lot more than my initial prediction of a winning bid of ten dollars. And then it hit me. If the designated church held a weekly service that lasted an hour, I would be attending church for the next year.

## MEETING THE MINISTER

The winning bidder turned out to be Jim Henderson, a former minister from Seattle and author of *Evangelism Without Additives*. Jim and I had exchanged brief e-mails earlier in the week. He had asked if I would be willing to attend a variety of churches, and of course, I replied that I would. One night after the auction, we spoke on the phone, discussing where and when he envisioned me fulfilling my end of the deal. He revealed that his Web site, www .off-the-map.org, had an unofficial slogan: "Helping Christians Be Normal." It turned out that Jim and I had both had experiences with Christians that turned us off. Jim mentioned that his ministry paid nonreligious people to attend church services and fill out surveys reflecting their thoughts. These surveys were used to help churches tweak their services and do a better job of getting the Christian message across.

Jim's motives for submitting the winning bid differed from what I had anticipated. I thought I would be sent to the winning bidder's choice of church every Sunday for the next year, and I would be preached to by the winner at every service. Jim, however, simply wanted me to go to church and write about it—not the same church for fifty weeks, though. Instead, he wanted me to go to no more than fifteen churches, fill out a survey for each one, and write about my visits on his Web site. In a sense, I would be a paid intern for his Web ministry. Between attending the churches, blogging, and doing media interviews (which I figured had already hit its peak), I would "earn" the money Jim had bid on eBay and fulfill my obligation.

## MY FIRST CATHOLIC MASS

Suzanne, the reporter who had been asking me questions via e-mail, said she wanted to observe me during my first church visit. She was writing for the *Wall Street Journal,* which meant my story would reach a nationwide audience. Since Jim was planning to join me, the three of us agreed to meet in Chicago the following Monday.

When I met Jim in person, I learned quite a bit about his efforts to improve how churches operate. In fact, I learned that he and I shared a core belief: churches can improve if they are willing to see themselves the way unchurched people see them. This has nothing to do with trying to change *what* churches teach but rather *how* they present the teachings of Christ. I knew I could identify a number of reasons nonreligious people were turned off by churches. And who knows, maybe something I would hear in church would cause me to reconsider the idea that God exists. The next day, I attended a Catholic Mass with Jim and Suzanne at the church I lived next to—Old Saint Pat's.

The architecture inside this historic church was beautiful, with stained-glass images and statues of people I didn't know high above the pews. I listened to the service and observed others at the noon Mass. They all kneeled and stood in unison, almost as if on cue. I tried to do everything I saw the congregation doing, except receive communion. When the service ended, the three of us regrouped at a nearby coffee shop. I had so many questions!

I shared my reactions, and Jim answered some of my questions, like who the statues represented and why we were going through certain motions. He also agreed with some of my criticisms—for example, the priest's monotone voice caused me to drift away in thought. When I heard Jim's explanation of the motions, such as why we were kneeling at specific times, I wondered if everyone else in the church knew the reasons. While I may have been a beat behind the rest, some churchgoers were a beat ahead. It was clear to me they were anticipating the next motion. They may have been genuine in their actions, but I was convinced some of them had repeated the same motions their entire lives without really thinking about what they were doing. But perhaps I was wrong. Maybe they honored God *by* going through those motions.

## The Convenience-Store Celebrity

Nearly a month after attending Old Saint Pat's, Suzanne called me again. The story would be running in the Thursday edition of the *Wall Street Journal*, two days away! That morning I woke up early and walked to a nearby convenience store to pick up a copy of the paper. On the front page of one of the most respected newspapers in the world, I saw the headline above the fold. It read: "On eBay, an Atheist Puts His Own Soul on the Auction Block." *Interesting choice of words,* I thought. When I flipped the paper over to read the article, a hand-drawn portrait of me stared back. No matter what else happened with this auction, it couldn't possibly get more surreal than this. The man working the cash register must have noticed my shock. He asked what I was reading, and I showed him the picture.

"That's me," I stammered.

"No way… Really?" He picked up another copy of the paper and saw the similarities. As I walked out of the store, I glanced back to see him showing the paper to a co-worker and pointing at me.

I went back to my apartment, remembering I hadn't even brushed my teeth or shaved. Normally, those tasks take me all of five minutes. This day, they took me nearly four hours. The phone would ring every time I lathered up. Radio stations, local television news, Fox News Channel, *Good Morning America, Anderson Cooper 360*, a game show that needed a contestant with an interesting story, a movie studio, an agent… They all wanted to talk to "the atheist who was going to church." It was immediately apparent that the concept of an atheist willing to question his own beliefs and discuss faith garnered tremendous interest.

The intrigue didn't come only from mainstream media. People who had read the *Wall Street Journal* article e-mailed me, praising my efforts and asking me to visit their churches. Some atheists wrote to say they enjoyed reading a story about a fellow atheist that didn't revolve around some legal issue or court case.

The *Chicago Sun-Times* (hey, maybe they found my press release!) also called, wanting to take my picture later that day inside a church. They were going to reprint the *Wall Street Journal* story and wanted something to add to it. Once again, Old Saint Pat's came to my rescue. The next morning, I woke up to find an e-mail from a stranger who had seen me in the *Sun-Times*. She asked what it's like to be famous. I wasn't sure what she was referring to…

I visited the same convenience store to pick up a copy of the newspaper. There I was again on the front page. It was me in the church balcony, with a headline underneath that read, "He Sold His Soul—for Just $504." I went to buy the paper, and the cashier just looked at me.

"It's you! Again! In the paper!"

"Yeah…" I still didn't know how to respond.

Within a week, articles about the auction had appeared on the *front page* of five newspapers, and the story was highlighted on countless radio and television programs. Given this great opportunity, I documented the journey on Jim Henderson's Web site (www.off-the-map.org) and made sure I took copious notes during each church visit. Readers started offering answers to the questions I was raising, just as I had hoped. As my blogging for Jim's Web site was coming to an end, I launched www.friendlyatheist.com as a place where I could continue to reflect on my churchgoing experiences as well as on issues that were important to me as an atheist. The name "friendly atheist" was appealing to me, since I rarely heard those two words used together. Perhaps a by-product of all the attention would be that the stereotypes so many people had about nonreligious people would be broken down.

## An Atheist with Soul

Despite my attempts to be known publicly as "the friendly atheist," I was still referred to in the media as "the guy who sold his soul." Other atheists were quick to point out the obvious irony: as an atheist, I didn't believe that an actual soul existed. But nevertheless, nearly every interview (often done alongside Jim Henderson) began with the question of why I decided to sell my soul, and every response I gave became an explanation of how I didn't *actually* do that. Frequently, the next words from the interviewer would be: "Uh-huh… So, Jim, how does it feel to own Hemant's soul?" A Web site that sells merchandise with secular slogans printed up items with the words: "Sold My Soul and All I Got Was Enough to Buy This Lousy T-Shirt." It seemed even atheists were having fun with the idea. Since I obviously could not fight the misinterpretation, I went with it. If people wanted to talk to the guy who sold his soul, I welcomed them, and used the occasion to explain what I was actually doing.

By the time my original blog (the predecessor to www.friendlyatheist .com) finally went up, I had attended five church services and had written about them on Jim Henderson's Web site. The feedback had been over-whelmingly positive even before the media picked up on the story. When I made comments on the blog about certain churches and what I experienced there, many of the pastors would log on to comment on my reaction to their sermons. One pastor actually thanked me for my critique. Another pastor, whose church I visited and wrote about on the Internet, later invited me to share the stage with him at all three of his weekend church services. He and I sat together in front of his congregation and discussed our respective views of faith, religion, and doubt. In front of hundreds of Christians at each service, we asked each other our most burning questions. (I'll go into detail about this unusual sermon featuring an atheist in chapter 10.)

Now that the news articles started to circulate throughout the country, my posts were being read by a much larger audience. In the meantime, I still had several church services I needed to attend. I had many more questions to ask and more outsider observations to make. The adventure was just beginning.

# The Reasons I Lost My Religion

## *But Under Other Circumstances, I Might Not Have*

I grew up a Chicago Cubs fan. To the surprise of many, however, that's not the reason I became an atheist. I won tickets to a Cubs game when I was in elementary school, and even though they lost the game (what else?), they won me over. What struck me as interesting was that there were so many fans in spite of the team's perennial ineptitude. Even as the team gave us hope every few years, they never could produce a World Series championship or even a pennant winner. Yet people like me still rooted for them. It would be much easier to cheer for a different team—one that wins (dare I mention the White Sox?). But it's not easy to shift your loyalties. Cubs fans stand by their team, *believing* that one day they will come through for us.

Following a baseball team has close parallels to following a certain religion. I became a Cubs fan because I saw a game and liked the team. But other fans began following baseball at a younger age and simply cheered for the same team their parents followed. Or else a friend or relative convinced them this was the team to watch.

Growing up in a minority religion, I felt a little like I was a part of the

Chicago Cubs of the religious world—I was rooting for a team that was never going to make it on the larger stage. My parents were Jains, so I followed their lead in religious matters. They said Jainism was the religion to support, and I loved and respected them too much to think otherwise. I didn't mind being a Jain; in fact, I valued many aspects of the faith. But Jainism certainly was not a World Series contender among religions in America.

Few people are born into an atheistic family. Most of us come to atheism years after we have been taught about a particular religion. Like other Jains, I grew up believing in heaven, hell, prayer, and so forth. Surprising to some, Jainism has no concept of a creator God. There's no omnipotent, benevolent God that watches over you. Jains do believe, however, in divine beings; these are the focus of their prayers.

The city of Chicago, where I was raised, boasts a significant Jain population as well as a beautiful Jain temple in Bartlett, a suburb to the west of the city. So I had a wonderful chance to learn and practice the religion as I grew up. You might think that today, as an atheist, I share a parallel belief with Jains, in that I don't believe in a creator God. But if you were to ask followers of Jainism if a God exists, many will say yes. It's too tempting a belief to reject, and the Jains I knew growing up believed someone was watching over them, even though this was not a part of actual Jain beliefs.

## THE BELIEFS OF MY CHILDHOOD

To see more clearly how Christianity comes across to a religious outsider, it might help you to know more about the beliefs I adopted as a child, and the reasons I later rejected those beliefs. You may even find that you agree with some of my reasoning. While I did not grow up Christian, I did grow up in a devoutly religious family. And when I chose to reject the idea of God, I was motivated in part by facets of my religion that didn't ring true.

The most prominent feature of Jainism is adherence to the values represented in the Five Vows: nonviolence, truth, nonstealing, celibacy (until marriage), and nonpossessiveness. These vows are so deeply respected that Mahatma Gandhi was said to be strongly influenced by Jainism. The vows led to his fervent belief in vegetarianism and nonviolent resistance. While other religions waged holy wars against one another, Jains were a peaceful, prosperous people.

Even as an atheist, I still adhere to these rules as best I can. For example, in keeping with the first vow (nonviolence), I remain a vegetarian. I also try not to spend money on products I don't need (nonpossessiveness). I am convinced society functions better when these five rules are followed. And on a personal level, adherence to the vows allows people to maintain a sense of self-control over unrestrained behavior. I'm sure you can appreciate the similarities to the Ten Commandments, with the exception that the Five Vows make no reference to a supreme being.

As a child, I said my prayers every morning and night feeling I was fortunate to be a part of the faith.[1] As a result of the positive impact of Jainism, I was hesitant to question the religion's *other* beliefs. *If we are right on the broad principles,* I reasoned, *we must also be right in the details.* I simply accepted what I was taught without thinking critically about it.

## DOUBTING KARMA AND REINCARNATION

When I did begin questioning my faith, I found that a number of core Jain beliefs failed to satisfy my curiosity. One of the key ideas in Jainism is that we have souls that have *always* existed. They have been here since the beginning of time and will always continue to exist. During our lives, our souls gather and shed karma, much like dust piling up on a shelf and then being swept away. When we perform bad deeds (both physically and mentally), the karma "particles" attach to our souls. We spend our lives trying to shed bad karma by performing good deeds.

We were taught that when someone dies, the soul simply inhabits another body in the process of reincarnation, taking with it the karma it had accumulated during the previous lifetime. If you succeed in shedding more bad karma than you had when you entered your previous life, then in your next life you would inhabit the body of someone in a *better position*. Hypothetically, a monkey that shed more of its karma could become a human in the next life. And a person born into the lowest caste in India could be born into a better caste during the next go-around.

However, good deeds were never enough. If a person wanted to attain full liberation from the cycle of reincarnations, he or she would have to withdraw from society and the material world entirely. After a seemingly endless cycle of reincarnations, if you shed *all* your bad karma, you would achieve enlightenment *(moksha)* and eventually become a *siddha*, freeing yourself from the cycle. This enlightened state is as close to God as Jainism gets. In theory at least, as a Jain, you have the power to *become* a heavenly being.

You could also go the other way, of course, by accumulating more bad karma during your lifetime. Hypothetically, murderers could end up as ants, or at the very least they could be in for many lifetimes of unhappiness.

Karma and reincarnation were two Jain teachings I rejected, once I took a closer look. The only evidence I ever heard in support of the reincarnation theory was that of children who supposedly knew what bodies they had occupied in previous lives, something I now consider to be just a young child's overactive imagination. I could easily provide a specific description of an imaginary person, and somewhere in the world someone probably did fit that profile at one point. And even as a kid, I started raising questions about karma. There was one question my friends and I would always (jokingly) ask each monk who came to visit our families: if we were stranded on an island with a bunch of animals, and the only way for us to stay alive was to eat them, should we do it? The answers varied widely. Strict Jains said we could never kill and eat an animal, while liberal Jains said we could eat meat, minimally, but only if we would use the now-extended part of our lives to work toward shedding the bad karma. Well, which view was right—the strict prohibition against eating animals, even when stranded on an island, or the more liberal allowance for limited eating of meat in dire circumstances?

One question always led to another. If our souls had always been in existence, how do Jains explain the exponential increase in the world's human population? If there are an unlimited number of souls, are there a certain number of souls off in some waiting room? And if the number of souls is limited, but the human population is increasing, would people at some time get only a fraction of the soul their ancestors had, in order to accommodate the expanding population? Or if people were reincarnated as lesser creatures, and there are billions of insects, are all the insects reincarnations of people who were bad in a previous life? Or does that explanation account for only *some* of the insects? And considering the number of insects on earth, if they are reincarnated people, wouldn't we have read in history books about these billions of horrible people, now deceased?

I never could get a straight answer.

## QUESTIONING ETERNITY

Because Jains believe that human souls are eternal, there has to be an eternal world for the souls to inhabit. Accordingly, the universe could not be created or destroyed.

Jainism breaks time into an infinite series of cycles, each of which consists of (essentially) six phases of rising happiness and six phases of declining happiness. (For those interested, we are currently in the fifth part of a declining-happiness half of a cycle, with just under twenty thousand years before phase six begins. This is supposed to explain why there are so many problems in the world. This also tells us that our descendents are in for a rough several millennia.)[2]

If there was a Jain belief that contradicted what I learned in school (such as the scientific understanding of a universe that is approximately 13.7 billion years old and certainly not eternal), I simply followed what I heard from my teachers. I assumed I didn't know everything about Jainism and that there must be a way to reconcile the differences. I still believed in the Five Vows, and that was enough for me to consider myself a true follower.

As I got older, however, I started examining the religious ideas I had been taught. I thought about the concept of Jain-time and couldn't find the basis for *how* we knew time was split up as Jainism said it was. And what about the belief that the earth had always existed? That went against everything in both the big bang theory *and* the biblical creation story! Someone had to be wrong. At least at school, my teachers explained the reasons behind scientists' thinking. The teaching of evolution went against not only the Jain teaching on eternity but also the idea of reincarnation. Why had we never discussed that discrepancy at the Jain temple?

## MY RELIGIOUS ROOTS

Choosing to question my beliefs was not an easy decision. I grew up in a devout family that was part of a larger, committed Jain community. My parents told me I was blessed to be born into a family that practiced such a great faith. At first I had no reason to doubt them.

Chicago is a focal point for Jainism—many Indians immigrated to the area in the 1970s—but there was not an official temple for Jains in the area until 1992. In the meantime, my parents wanted a way to teach me and my sister about our religion. Their friends wanted to do the same with their children. The one aspect of our Indian culture they did not want us to lose was Jainism.

To keep the teachings alive, the adults began to hold once-a-month meetings called *jaap* at each others' houses. At these get-togethers, several families would spend one hour chanting mantras and singing songs of praise. In addition, there would be time for the children—individually—to recite their religious knowledge. Even after our temple was finally built in 1992, our small community had grown so close that we continued holding the Sunday *jaap*.

At first, I didn't mind the gatherings. It was a chance to see my friends, and we knew the one hour of prayer (though sometimes tedious) would be followed by several hours of talking and catching up with each other, playing basketball outside, or watching the Bears play football.

It was at a *jaap* we attended when I was twelve that my family announced to our close friends that we would be moving to Tennessee. My father had lost his job but had been offered a position in Knoxville. Although I did not want to move, I realized I could still keep in touch with my close friends by writing letters, and we would surely make frequent visits back to Chicago.

## A JAIN IN EAST TENNESSEE

Knoxville was warm and welcoming, but as far as I could tell, we were one of the only Jain families in the entire city. After we moved, I put religion on the back burner, choosing instead to focus on school and after-school activities. If the topic of religion ever came up, though, it turned out that no one in any of my classes had heard of Jainism. And trying to explain my beliefs was a futile, often embarrassing exercise, so I kept my religion to myself. But a question I had thought about before stuck with me: if Jainism really is true, wouldn't everyone know at least a *little* about it?

Since political distinctions and religious affiliations weren't issues that stood out to me, it was only in retrospect that I realized how heavily my school environment was influenced by Christianity. No one tried to convert me, but I'm amazed now that I never paid much attention when students wore crosses to school or said they couldn't hang out on weekends because they had to attend a church function.

Taking that into account, it was a remarkable coincidence that my closest friend in Knoxville—a girl I had met through acting in our school's plays—turned out to be an agnostic. Jeannette and I never spoke too much about religion, but we both knew we were in the minority. (Jains and agnostics weren't highly visible at our school, which is perhaps one of the reasons the two of us bonded.) When she would explain to me why she wasn't a religious person, her logic made sense. I didn't agree with her at the time, but the idea that you couldn't *really* know if God existed, so why stake a claim to knowing the answer one way or the other, was a valid one.

When I completed eighth grade, I was eager to begin high school. I had spent the summer with my close friends, and we would often discuss our plans for the next year. We knew we'd be involved in theater and the forensics team, and we picked our schedule based on which friends would be in the same classes. So it was devastating when I learned that my dad's employer was laying off people and my dad would have to find another job. He was able to find work in the south suburbs of Chicago—a far cry from the northwestern suburb of Schaumburg where we had lived before.

My family moved a week before high school started.

Instead of the excitement I had built up over attending Farragut High School in Knoxville, I was forced to enter Carl Sandburg High School in Orland Park, Illinois. The idea that I would have to restart what had taken me two years to do—make new friends, find a niche—was overwhelming. If the other students at Carl Sandburg were anything like me, they already had their cliques. And why would they choose to include me?

## THE SPROUTING SEEDS OF DOUBT

In my mind, moving was *obviously* the worst thing that could ever happen to me. Even though I had tried to live a good life, I was being punished. Why would God make my life so wonderful in Tennessee, only to take it away so quickly? I tried to find a rationale that God was using, but I came up empty. I began to think that if God existed, I wouldn't be put in this situation.

In retrospect, it's easy to see that my line of thinking was off base. Any believer could have pointed out that God did this for a reason. Maybe I would be even better off than before in a new location! Maybe Knoxville was just preparation for this new adventure. God might have something tremendous in store for me back in Illinois.

They would've been right. Attending Carl Sandburg High School *was* a blessing in disguise. The new friends I (quickly) made, the teachers who influenced me during the next four years, and the groups I was involved with (still including theater and the speech team) were life-changing in a way I could never have anticipated. But when I was fourteen, I didn't know any of this. My doubts began to take over. I no longer knew if God really existed. For the first time, I began to seriously question my faith.

What started out as casual questions now became much more troubling. If I couldn't get answers—and by answers, I meant the same reliable, reasonable answers from different Jain scholars to all my questions—did that mean no one knew the real answers? And if they didn't know the answers, how could they claim Jainism was right?

The parables of my religion also started raising new questions. One has to do with the *tirthankar* Mahavir. (A *tirthankar* is a figure who has achieved enlightenment and spreads the Jain message to others.) Legend had it that when Mahavir was walking through a forest, he encountered a poisonous snake named Chandakaushik. Mahavir didn't flinch at the sight of the snake, and this lack of fear threw off Chandakaushik, who was accustomed to frightening anyone who crossed his path. The snake, in anger, decided to bite Mahavir's toe. When he did, he was shocked to see pure, white milk come out. Mahavir, still peaceful and calm, told the snake nonviolence was the best way to live and then continued on his way. The snake was moved by these words and heeded the message. When the snake died, he went to heaven.

As a teenager, I realized how absurd this story sounded. How did we know the story was true if no one else was there? How did milk come out of someone's toe? Did Jainism just copy the "evil snake" bit from the Bible or was it the other way around? Or did we all get it from somewhere else?

I have heard the idea that since much of ancient India was illiterate, Jain teachers may have created these stories to convey the messages of Jainism. They were never meant to be taken literally. However, as they were passed down from one generation to the next, each story took on a life of its own and *became* true for those hearing it. If that was the case, though, there was never an indication in any of the texts that the stories were fiction. It seemed that many people in the Jain community, including my parents, just accepted the ideas. Jains seemed to have the right ideas but the wrong reasoning behind them.

I still attended *jaap,* and I still went to temple celebrations, but with a vastly different mind-set. Every song and prayer now became mere words on a page. I began to look forward to the monthly meetings only to see my friends. If I was an hour late and missed the prayer portion, so be it.

## THE NIGHT I LOST MY RELIGION

I was unsettled by the thoughts that were gaining ground in my head—that maybe the whole idea of Jainism was made up. And maybe there really were no such things as reincarnation…or karma…or heaven and hell…or God. I would stay up late at night using the Internet to research these ideas and various people who shared my thoughts. Each question led me to Web sites that seemed to talk about atheism, and while I was hesitant to even associate myself with that word, the writers whose work I was reading had the same types of questions I did, but pertaining to other religions. And they all came to the conclusion that God was a man-made idea. The more I read, the more sense it made. But I wasn't ready to give up on my faith just yet.

The turning point came during the holiest part of the Jain year. For my family's sect of Jainism, it was a period of eight days in September known as *Paryushana*. Many Jains fast for one of these eight days—no food, no drink, all day. Devout Jains will go so far as to fast for eight days straight, with the sole exception being the allowance of water that has been boiled first (so bacteria will not continue to reproduce and die). It's a testament of willpower to not eat at all, and it is only after the eighth day that Jains who fast take their first bite of food. My mother usually practiced a combination of the different fasting methods and would eat only once a day for all eight days.

My sister, when she was eleven, wanted to be a "devout Jain" by fasting for all eight days. At her age this would pose a serious health risk, but no one discouraged her from fasting. Quite the opposite: a celebration was planned for her, as well as the other Jains who fasted, to be held when the eight days were over.

To my sister's credit, she made it through the week with only water passing her lips. While she was very weak at the end, she slowly regained her strength with no permanent health effects. But for me, my little sister's being allowed to endure a dangerous eight-day fast was the last straw. While I had been inching toward atheism, in the past I wouldn't dare call myself the *a* word. I felt it was an ugly word. But at that point I became comfortable with using *atheist* to describe myself.

I wasn't sure how to make the change at first. How does one simply become an atheist? There was no induction ceremony, so I simply went to bed. However, for the first time in my life, I did so without saying my prayers. The next morning I woke up and checked myself in the mirror, looking for scars or other telltale marks that would show God was angry with me. But they weren't there. Nothing had changed other than my thoughts. Remarkably, I had left the Chicago Cubs of the religion world and signed on with a team that wasn't even in the same league! It was the first major decision I had made without anyone telling me what I should do. Unfortunately, I had to keep it to myself. I was too afraid to tell anyone in my family that I no longer believed in Jainism.

## Seeking a Compelling Reason to Believe

As I think about my de-conversion, it occurs to me that if certain things had been different, I might have held on to my belief in God. In fact, any religion that wants to keep people believing should do one simple thing: instead of limiting religious teaching to matters of what to do and how to do it, tell people *why* they are saying certain words, performing certain rituals, and adhering to certain beliefs. The reasons behind religious beliefs and practices must be made clear, and they must stand alone. Do historical records exist that confirm the religious view? Does evidence exist in the physical world that corroborates assertions made in the sacred writings of that religion? What validity do these things have outside the religious world? Don't rely on reasons such as, "This is what Catholics have always done," or, "The Bible says we should do this, so we do it." For teenagers and others who seek concrete answers to their spiritual questions, the biblical story alone is not enough. If it's not possible for Bible teachers to cross-reference biblical explanations with nonbiblical sources, many teens will reject their faith as they grow older.

I sought evidence that would give me reasons to continue believing, and I no longer think it is possible to find such reasons.

Many atheists I know started out as Christians—often as evangelical Christians. Even when they grew older and had the capacity to understand the reasons behind their beliefs, many still were not given any reasons. The ones who did hear reasons found them unsatisfactory, and their own research revealed no logical explanations for their practices, so they decided to become atheists. In my case, the list of recitable mantras kept growing while the reasons for saying them came to a standstill. And when I finally heard the explanations, they were not convincing.

Born-again Christians can attest to the fact that when they accept Christ into their lives, their world changes dramatically. Everything is now seen through a new set of lenses. The same thing happened to me when I rejected religion. It was incredible how pervasive religion had become in my life and how differently I had to think now that I wasn't religious. As an atheist, I had a completely new outlook on life.

## LIFE WITHOUT GOD

The hardest part about becoming an atheist was considering all the implications of a no-God world. If He really does not exist, then all the prayers I had said would have been for nothing. And all those children dying in Third World countries weren't suffering the consequences of a bad previous life; they were just unlucky. And an even bigger question: what was the meaning of life if not to reach heaven? I didn't know then. But maybe we didn't need a predestined purpose. It seemed that all religions were trying to answer questions they didn't have the answers to. What was so wrong with not knowing? Why couldn't we just try to improve our lives, be happy, and make things better for future generations?

When your worldview starts to make sense, you feel a sense of power. You want to turn to people and shout, "You don't get it, but I do!" Of course, I didn't "know" for sure. But it sure felt that way at first.

It was only after I became an atheist that I began to really question my ethical framework and my behaviors. Since Jainism focused on nonviolence, did being vegetarian still make sense? Of course it did. It was still wrong to kill animals, because they were as alive as I was, with families of their own. Would I still tell the truth? Obviously, yes. If everyone lied to one another, our society would never be able to accomplish anything. By telling the truth, others would trust us and help us in times of need; they would know we were not trying to take advantage of them. Would I steal? Not a chance. Someone's life would be changed for the worse if I were a thief, and I didn't want to hurt anybody. My ethics and morals didn't fade away when religion was out of my life. Even though I may have learned my morals because of religion, I could still make sense of those morals when Jainism was out of the picture.

In the past several years, I have found that many other atheists share a similar story to mine. So many of us, when we reached the preteen and early teen years—often referred to as reaching the Age of Reason—questioned our commitment to faith. This pattern of questioning is probably the best argument I know in favor of atheism. How can so many people from such different backgrounds come to the same conclusions without being targeted by an organized effort to indoctrinate them against religion? You hear of people in remote, isolated villages learning about Christ through the work of missionaries. However, many people across the globe reject religion in favor of atheism without being preached to by atheist missionaries. It just happens—and the way it happens is remarkably similar among those who were not raised to adopt atheism.

In fairness, however, I must mention that the Age of Reason can also result in the opposite outcome. A period of questioning one's faith can lead a person to have an even deeper connection to God. The preteen and teenage years are some of the most volatile for religious identity, and which side a child lands on depends largely on what he or she experiences at this point in life. Parents can't control their children's life experiences, of course. But they can do more to help answer their children's questions.

At age fourteen I was asking questions. When the answers failed to satisfy me, I searched elsewhere for different answers and found wisdom in atheism. And I am far from alone in that experience.

Accepting the existence of God might seem to be a no-brainer, a belief that is easily adopted by any right-thinking person. You might even think belief in God is something we're born with. But I think we're born *without* any knowledge of God and are taught by our parents or other influential people that God exists. In my case, I was taught a religion during my childhood and then chose a different path when I was a teenager.

Even though everyone in my family was a practicing Jain, all of a sudden at age fourteen I was supporting the other team. And as I got older, I continued to venture even further into the world of atheism.

# Getting to Know an Atheist

## Most Nonreligious People Don't Fit the Stereotypes

Christians tell certain stories that capture important aspects of their belief system. Atheists often do the same. One story that illustrates an important principle for nonreligious people involves a battle between the Wind and the Sun. Each one argued that it was more powerful. The Wind contended that it had the ability to move ships across oceans, destroy cities, and cause bridges to collapse. The Sun countered that it could start fires, help crops grow, and power entire buildings.

The Wind and Sun decided to settle the matter once and for all. Spotting a young girl walking to school, they decided to compete to see who could make the girl take off her jacket. The wiser Sun, knowing he would easily be the victor, sat back and watched while the Wind went to work. The Wind's strategy was to blow the jacket off the girl. It blew harder and harder hoping the girl would give up the struggle and stop clutching her jacket. Yet every time the Wind blew, the girl only clung more tightly. No matter what the Wind did, it could not find a way to separate the girl from her jacket.

Next, it was the Sun's turn. It simply shone as brightly as it could. As the girl felt the heat building up, she quickly removed her jacket. The Sun won the contest.

Why might atheists appreciate this story? Because it shows that persuasion is more effective than coercion. The Wind, trying to force a result, lost to the Sun's gentle approach. The story of the Wind and the Sun reflects the general religious environment I observed around me, especially when I entered college. At the time, there was much more Wind than Sun. It seemed that most religious organizations on campus were out to convert me by coercion. Not every religious person used these tactics, certainly, but many organized groups made no secret of their intentions. Several times on my state university campus I would pass a table where students would ask if I knew where I was going when I died. My response of "nowhere" never went over well. And since I wanted to be polite, I'd stay and listen to a lecture explaining how I was doomed unless I came to their Bible study.

Other times, I was asked to take a short quiz. I enjoy trivia, so I was eager to do it, until I saw I was being tested on my biblical knowledge. Still, I would answer the questions correctly (atheists often know the Bible pretty well). I would then be invited to attend a Christian small group. At that point I would tell the students I was an atheist, which only made them work harder to get me to come. It was always an awkward situation. A close friend of mine, who was not an atheist, would tell these students she *was* one simply because she was irritated by their attempts to convert everyone in their path.

I didn't run into this confrontational approach in high school. During that time, I was exposed to a great variety of religions. My friends ran the gamut of religiosity—Christians, Jews, Hindus, Muslims. Everyone had a chance to share and learn from one another. I learned, for instance, that a Christian friend from the Middle East was a minority in a mostly Muslim country, and her relatives back home faced hardships as a result. A Hindu friend and I disagreed on the idea of an afterlife but found common ground when noting that religious-based fighting between Hindus and Muslims in

India only resulted in devastation for both sides, regardless of who "won." I went to the flagpole one morning in September with my Christian friends during the annual prayer event. I wanted to support them and observe the prayers. It was obvious that individually we held conflicting beliefs. But for the most part, common sense and friendship took precedence over trying to prove that one view was right and the others were wrong.

## RELIGION ON CAMPUS

Prior to entering college, I hadn't been part of an organized secular group. Even though I had never faced significant opposition because of my beliefs, I discovered that other atheists weren't always that lucky. And because atheists are a minority in American society, I felt a strong desire to meet other nonreligious people. I knew only a few atheists in high school, and surprisingly, I found even fewer in college. It was puzzling: the high-profile Christians who were quoted in the media claimed public universities were a bastion of secular thought…and yet at the University of Illinois at Chicago (UIC) I wasn't meeting anyone who shared a secular mind-set. One poll I read said nonreligious people made up more than 14 percent of the U.S. population,[1] so I knew there must be other atheists on campus. The question was how we could spot each other.

The first place I checked was the office for student organizations. I suspected that a group for nonreligious students had already been established since there were groups for just about everything else. It turned out UIC had not a single atheist club, but it did have twenty-seven religious groups! And most of them were Christian. I was stunned. Wouldn't it be wiser to have one large, united group to achieve a strong Christian presence on campus? I considered reasons for the different factions. Maybe some students enjoyed large-group worship while others preferred the more intimate smaller gatherings. Or maybe the splits reflected the different denominations represented among

Christians. Maybe some students wanted their own groups so they could worship according to their cultural traditions. I could understand creating separate groups along these lines, even if I felt they were detrimental to the ultimate goals of most groups—building a sustainable community.

But why was there no group for atheist students? At first I thought my university must be an anomaly. But years later, when I checked the ratio between Christian groups and secular groups at other public universities, I found UIC to be typical. I looked up the list of the ten largest universities (based on student population) in the country and found one of the largest schools, the University of Texas at Austin, had seventy-four Christian groups alone! I couldn't come up with seventy-four reasons Christians could have for needing separate groups. When I looked at the names of the organizations, the apparent reasons for maintaining different groups seemed irrelevant. It appeared that graduate students, lawyers, athletes, and various fraternities needed their own separate meetings. And Christians weren't alone in this regard. Islamic, Jewish, and even Buddhist students had several groups each at that campus. Yet there was only one group for atheists. The ratios simply did not reflect the religious demographics in the country. If more than 14 percent of the national population shared a nonreligious outlook, then shouldn't there have been several atheist groups on the UT–Austin campus? Or at the very least, more than one? When I checked other public universities, I found a similar lopsided ratio of Christian groups to organizations for nonreligious students.

I wondered if this was just a public-school phenomenon. I used the 2004 *U.S. News & World Report* list of the ten best schools in the nation—mostly private schools—to see if the ratio was different. Even at Harvard University, which had a vastly smaller student population than the public universities, I still found the number of Christian groups ranging in the double digits, while the number of atheist (or other secular, freethinking, humanist, and so on) groups remained at one. At every school I checked, the number of organizations for non-Christian religions was no more than a handful, but still more than one in most cases. Each school was dominated by Christian organizations, and not a single school I looked at had more than one secular group.

With this in mind, I knew that before I graduated I wanted to help start a campus group at UIC. Christian groups certainly had a right to form (and divide themselves up, if they wanted to), but there also needed to be at least one strong, united organization for nonbelievers, a group that would serve those students who were looking for an alternative to religion.

## How to Find Atheists

While starting any campus organization required little more than time and paperwork, I knew I had an uphill battle in trying to launch a *successful* campus group for atheists. Only a small fraction of the undergraduates lived on our campus—the rest of the students commuted daily. Also, many students held jobs. Since I had virtually no budget to start a new group, any event would need to be held at night to secure free meeting space, and as a result it would be much more difficult to attract a crowd.

Regardless, I spent the summer after my first year of college learning how to establish and lead a student organization. I needed to find a faculty-member sponsor, but I didn't know if any of my professors were atheists. And it didn't seem like a question I could just come out and ask. I searched my school's Web site for the term *atheist* and found only a paper discussing religion, with atheism as a focus. I didn't know who the author was, but I wrote to him asking if he knew any professors who could help me out. As it turned out, the author was a graduate student who knew a number of professors who might be interested.

We continued to correspond, sharing book lists and discussing our backgrounds; it was great to finally talk to another atheist on campus. A few weeks later, he informed me that someone else—an undergrad named Kaye—had also written to him saying she wanted to start a group! Kaye and I quickly set the group in motion.

By the beginning of my second year of college, we assigned student officer positions, filled out the requisite forms, and created a name: Students WithOut Religious Dogma (SWORD). We advertised the group by chalking the campus sidewalk with meeting announcements, sending e-mails to other student organizations whose members might be interested in attending our meetings, and putting flyers on bulletin boards. Many of our flyers were ripped down by other students, so it was reasonable to think there was opposition to our group. Still, when we held our first few meetings, those who attended seemed to feel pride and relief in conversing in an uncensored and safe environment.

## THE ANTIATHEIST BIAS

Christians might not think about this very much, but atheists are discriminated against in the United States. Sometimes it comes out in overt ways, such as being denied a job or a promotion based on a person's commitment to atheism. The name Herb Silverman may not ring many bells outside his home state of South Carolina, but he is a personal hero of mine. In 1990, Silverman, a college professor, discovered that his state's constitution required public officeholders (both elected and appointed) to affirm the existence of "the Supreme Being" (that is, God). Silverman felt the requirement violated the U.S. Constitution. Whatever happened to the idea of "holding no religious test for public office"? So he ran for governor (he was known as "the candidate without a prayer"). Silverman lost the race; however, still wanting to serve in a public office, he applied to be a notary public. Of the thirty thousand applicants approved in South Carolina between 1991 and 1993, Silverman was the only person rejected. Finally, in 1997, the state's supreme court decided his rights had been violated, and the state law was overturned. He is now a notary public.

Silverman's story and others like it help explain why the founding of SWORD was welcomed by secular students at UIC. Nonreligious students could now exchange ideas without fear of being ostracized or chastised. Those who attended our meetings mostly consisted of atheists and agnostics. If you are a Christian, it might surprise you to know we looked forward to learning from religious friends, who were always invited to participate. In fact, two students from the nearby Moody Bible Institute often attended our meetings because they enjoyed the discussions. My close friend Anne, a leader of a Catholic group on campus, also attended many of our meetings, both to support what I was doing and because she, too, appreciated the dialogue. We began to hold more discussions for all faiths, dealing with subjects such as death and the possibility of heaven.

Before this, most religious discussions I observed at school were limited to students from the same religious background. SWORD was bringing together groups of people who held a variety of beliefs. Instead of arguing about our differences, we were talking openly about diverse beliefs and often coming to consensus about our commonalities. For example, during a discussion on religious wars, we found that while certain students felt their religion was on the right side of the war, they would still concede that peace was a better option. No one wanted to see their religion resort to violence as a way to make a point. In all these discussions, the goal was conversation rather than conversion. And that was the key to our success.

In order to secure a larger budget to finance more events, Kaye suggested we affiliate our group with a national secular organization. I had no idea one even existed. She said she knew people from the Secular Student Alliance (SSA), an umbrella organization for atheist and agnostic college groups. While the SSA had a central headquarters, it was visible mostly due to its chapters that operated on college campuses across the country.

After SWORD became a chapter of SSA, we applied for grants to fund a variety of projects: bringing secular speakers to our school, hosting debates, giving pamphlets and books to interested students like the religious groups often did, and even serving free food at our meetings to encourage more students to participate.

During the two years I was a leader of SWORD, we brought in numerous speakers. The most notable was Michael Newdow, the atheist who had attempted to remove the words *under God* from the Pledge of Allegiance. He spoke to the UIC community just weeks after he argued his case before the U.S. Supreme Court. After giving a talk about his story and sharing what he had gone through personally (he had received death threats from extremists in the religious community), he opened the floor to questions. Students who disagreed with his stance challenged his views and his cause, and those who supported him praised his efforts. There were no protests and not even any mean-spirited remarks. It was simply a chance to hear a side of the story that wasn't told very often in the news media.

SWORD also sponsored a debate between an atheist lawyer and a Catholic professor on the existence of God, which brought in several hundred people, larger than any crowd I had seen at other UIC events. The questions the audience posed during the postevent discussions were inquisitive without being hostile. I didn't care if people were being won over to "my side." I just loved giving people an opportunity to discuss the controversial subject of religion openly and enthusiastically.

As I met leaders of secular student groups on other campuses, I found that some of them faced daunting challenges. Predominantly in the Bible Belt states, atheist organizations often struggled to hold events without Christian protesters holding up the event or interrupting their activities. I could understand if Christians wanted to come to atheist events to ask questions, or even if they chose to write a letter to the campus newspaper espousing their own views. But their hostile actions seemed to go against the Christian principles they were trying to promote. What were they so worried about, that some-one would hear a new idea?

## DISUNITY AMONG CHRISTIANS

Because atheists make up a minority of the population, we tend to stick to-gether. The relatively small number of national atheist organizations are quick to support one another. But one thing does stand out when you talk to vari-ous Christians, or even if you do nothing more than casually observe Chris-tians. The incredible range of views and beliefs among Christian groups is mind-boggling. It intrigues me and sometimes confuses me. I have often asked Christians why there is such a diversity of thought among them con-cerning their religious views, and the response I get often is dismissive: "That other person isn't practicing the *right kind* of Christianity."

Even if various Christians differ over the particular traditions they follow, I would expect them to show support for one another. All Christians follow the same underlying principles, right? When I attend a large convention of atheists, they seem to be more cohesive in their support for one another than what I have seen among Christians. Sure, we don't share *all* the same opin-ions, but we respect one another and enter into respectful debate over our dif-ferences. In atheism, there isn't a definitive right or wrong answer when it comes to political or social issues. We defend and concede points as we flesh out reasonable arguments for each side of an issue. The only belief that is common among us is our nonbelief in God and the supernatural.

Atheists are concerned voters. We're patriotic Americans (who do exist in foxholes).[2] We care about our country and our communities. We're just like religious Americans…without the religion. We donate time as well as money when natural disasters occur. We donate blood. There are several charitable groups made up of atheists, such as the Richard Dawkins Foundation for Science & Reason (www.richarddawkins.net), whose mission includes the goal of providing resources for atheists so they can contribute money to charities worldwide that do not proselytize those they help.

Of course, no community can achieve constant harmony or unbroken unity. As I got to know the secular organizations and their leaders, I witnessed firsthand the tensions that exist between some secular groups. Through conversations with other leaders, I learned there were groups that historically did not cooperate with the others, but that is slowly changing. In fact, when the news media credited Christian political activism as a force in determining the outcome of the 2004 presidential election, the heads of nearly every major secular organization met to discuss communal goals and how to achieve them. This has since become an annual event.

If you are a Christian, you probably aren't aware of the obstacles non-religious Americans face on a daily basis. We atheists, agnostics, and other freethinkers have to work hard to defend our rights, especially our constitutional right to "not believe."

Before I invite you to go to church with me, starting in chapter 5, I'd like to help you see things through a religious outsider's eyes. After you look at the world as I see it every day, you will understand better my observations and reactions to what I experienced when I started visiting churches.

# What the Nonreligious Believe

## *An Atheist's Primary Conflicts with Religious Teaching*

Every April for nearly forty years now, thousands of people have descended on the city of Stevens Point, Wisconsin, for a weekend-long trivia tournament—the largest trivia tournament in the world. A local college radio station runs the competition; they read trivia questions over the air and play songs in between while teams call the station, giving the answer to the latest question. Tournament officials allocate points based on how many teams answer each question correctly.

While the trivia tournament heats up, a number of "side" competitions also take place. One of the more interesting involves a scavenger hunt. At a certain time, a few members from each team arrive in their cars at a designated starting point. As they listen to the radio station, they hear a set of clues designed to guide them to a particular destination. If they reach the destination within the proper time frame, they receive a stamp worth a set number of points.

An example of the driving clues given over the radio might be: "Pass the chasm and continue running after the money. Then take the second right. Go past the sun and make a left. Go straight past the two silvers and collect your stamp." The clues are symbolic and not always easy to decipher. As the competitors begin the scavenger hunt, there is usually a line of cars heading the same direction, and it's tempting to follow the crowd to find the clues.

> We're crossing a bridge—that must be the chasm underneath—and that sign says there's an ATM in the store to our left—the money! Let's take the second right turn we see. There's a yellow letter *o* in that store's logo… Is that supposed to be the sun? Maybe…make a left. Does anyone see anything silver? Where are we…?

It's easy to fall in line with the others. Even if you missed one of the clues, it's reasonable to think others in front of you caught it. They couldn't *all* be wrong, could they? But at some point, you reach a dead end. You can't find what you're looking for, but you're certain you've followed the right path up to this point. The answer *must* be here…but where?

Some teams realize sooner than others that something went wrong. They drive back to the starting point and rethink their path. They are more careful the second time, keeping their eyes open for clues they missed earlier. This time they ignore the cars in front of them, and when they finally reach the end point, it's easy to see that previously they had taken the wrong road.

> A chasm…? Hey! There's a Gap store up ahead. But the ATM was back there…wait! There's a Chase bank sign to our right! That's perfect! Make the second right! We're by a cemetery… Where are we going to find a sun here? All I see are gravestones. In fact, there's one with Jesus on a cross… Oh! I get it! They didn't mean *sun*, they meant *Son*! Make a left! All I see down this dark road are speed-limit signs. We have to drive twenty-five miles per hour… Isn't a silver anniversary your twenty-fifth? I see two signs like that! We did it!

It makes perfect sense in retrospect.

This is the best way I can describe how I felt once I became an atheist. People often assume I hate God or that I habitually push God away, or even that I resist imposing a moral code on myself. The truth is, those sentiments are completely unrelated to my beliefs. When I examined Jainism, the religion of my childhood, I could no longer follow the logic in its most fundamental claims. I kept hitting dead ends. But when I reexamined life using the reasoning of atheists, everything started to fall into place.

## QUESTIONS RAISED BY RELIGIOUS TEACHINGS

Religion tries to answer unanswered (and sometimes unanswerable) questions, ones philosophers have struggled with for millennia. Atheism also seeks answers to questions, but when we don't know an answer, we admit it. Atheists believe in the Big Bang, for instance. The calculations indicating an expanding universe that is nearly 14 billion years old—and the existence of cosmic microwave background radiation—tell us there was this bang, even if we can't replicate it in a lab. But we don't know for sure how it began, because that is beyond our ability to calculate or observe. What launched the Big Bang, what was the catalyst, and why did it occur? Without the ability to observe or test conditions as they existed before the Big Bang, any explanations as to the origin of the universe lie outside the realm of our knowledge. Sure, a number of hypotheses speculate on what *could've* happened, but no single theory I have read is supported by more evidence than any other. Still, I appreciate the honesty of an answer that admits "we don't know for certain." Rather than a dead end, it's the beginning of several different paths, each of which can be explored further, and each of which may have some element of truth to it.

Being willing to leave certain questions unanswered, such as the atheist response to the question of what caused or preceded the Big Bang, is far different than doubt. Doubt for me had to do with giving serious consideration to certain religious beliefs and teachings and finding they heightened confusion rather than explaining life as I knew it. I have given careful thought to various Christian teachings, even though I was raised in an Eastern religion. For example, there is the belief that murderers who "accept Jesus" will go to heaven when they die, but someone like Mahatma Gandhi, who used nonviolence to combat India's caste system and to fight for the country's independence, went to hell because he was a Hindu and not a Christian. The Christian explanation for this is that God says we are all sinners and only through Christ's death and resurrection can we be redeemed. The murderer who accepts Jesus is taking advantage of God's offer of redemption, while Gandhi didn't. The conflict I have with this explanation is that it contradicts common-sense notions of justice. How could someone who took another human's life reap greater eternal rewards than a person who dedicated his life to helping others?

The idea of an afterlife is also troubling. The atheist view of death, which is that death is the cessation of existence, makes much more sense to me—considering the fact that I've never met anyone who died and then came back to verify what happened after death. The life that matters is this life, the one on Earth, the one we know for sure exists. So it makes sense that we should spend *this* life working together and helping one another. We'd be wasting our precious time on Earth by constantly opposing or attacking one another.

I never understood people who said that without God we would be grossly immoral people, killing, raping, and looting. (I've never seen any of those activities at any atheist gathering I've attended.) Atheists can respond to this claim by saying, "If you need God to prevent you from killing others, I'm *glad* you're religious. I can be good without God." Treating others with respect is good for the other person, as well as the person who shows respect. Furthermore, it's good for society as a whole. You don't need a religion to tell you being kind and respectful is the best way to live.

I find that atheism gives me honest and logical answers, admitting at times that it can't answer every question. Meanwhile, the claims made by a variety of religious faiths require me to believe things my reasoning cannot reconcile.

## WHAT THE NONRELIGIOUS BELIEVE

To help dispel the false stereotypes many religious people have of atheists, it's important to understand the way atheists think and what we believe. I recognize that my experiences do not reflect those of every other atheist or of all nonreligious people, but I'm convinced we experience and approach life with some common underlying themes.

Being an atheist involves more than mere denial of God's existence. An atheist's outlook impacts all aspects of life. There is a shared set of beliefs as well as less-essential issues that nonreligious people can choose whether or not to adhere to. Just as there is tremendous variety among Christians, not all secular people are the same. You would be in error if you called a Lutheran a Presbyterian. Likewise, some humanists may get upset if you describe them as atheists. No one wants to be stuck with an inaccurate label.

It's difficult to encapsulate an entire belief (or disbelief) system. Moreover, even the terms *disbelief* or *nonbelief* are often mistaken to mean that people like me have no beliefs at all, instead of merely lacking *religious* beliefs. But the following simple definitions should serve our purposes.

- *Atheists* are people who don't believe in a God, gods, or the supernatural.
- *Agnostics* hold that an answer on these matters one way or the other cannot be found and, thus, to varying degrees, they don't take a stand.
- *Freethinkers,* when faced with any claim, rely on their own reason and experience—so they may or may not be religious.

- *Humanism* encompasses the ideas of atheists, agnostics, and nontheistic freethinkers as it pursues moral and ethical values derived from human empathy, reason, and experience. Some humanists are religious in a purely social sense, in that they join with a community of other humanists for ceremonial activities and the celebration of special occasions. Secular humanists, by contrast, reject or have no interest in this expression of their philosophy.

I could define myself by many of these words, though *atheist* has always resonated most with me. To help you see the world as an atheist sees it, it might help to consider a few religious themes and questions and look at the way an atheist typically approaches those issues.

## Prayer

When I became an atheist, I noticed religion everywhere I went, perhaps because at the time I was searching for signs of confirmation or denial of my new belief paradigm. For example, in high school I observed many of my classmates praying before taking a big test. Believing that prayer had no actual effect, I began to think, *Why didn't they just study? What good will prayer do if you don't know the material?* When the test papers were returned, those students never seemed to do much better than the students who didn't pray. The same type of thing happened when I acted in theatrical productions, where some students would pray before a big performance. After months of rehearsal, I reasoned, there wasn't much more an actor could do but to get on stage and play his or her part.

## Suffering and Misfortune

When I saw students pass me in the hallways using wheelchairs, I didn't know how to deal with the injustice. When I was religious, my first thought—by habit—was that God had a special purpose for those people. But as an atheist, I wasn't so sure. Maybe they just had some bad luck. Or bad genes. I had the same feeling about students with special needs. When I thought of people with autism or those with Down syndrome, it seemed they were simply the unfortunate carriers of a genetic mishap. The lone bright side was that if science could explain the problem, science might eventually resolve the problem.

## Childrearing

When I thought about having children in the future, religion suddenly loomed as an issue that could have a major impact. I wasn't sure if I wanted my children to be raised as atheists—I knew it wouldn't be easy for them. Then again, atheism was the truth for me, and that idea was what I would want to pass on to my children. If I were dating a religious person, and we got serious about each other, would I consider raising our future children in her religion? No, I wouldn't. Suddenly, the thought was more complex than I imagined. At the time, I could simply put off trying to find a solution, since I didn't plan on having kids for a long time.

But now that I'm approaching an age when I could be getting married and having kids, I can no longer avoid the topic. There are some religious ideas I wouldn't mind my children learning and others I am against. If it meant a lot to my wife to get our children baptized, fine. To me, baptism is just water. But if our children were required to attend catechism classes and learn what I consider to be irrelevant rituals, I would oppose such practices being taught to them. Like other interreligious couples, we would need to work out certain compromises.

## Cultural Traditions

In regard to raising children, another issue that may concern atheist parents more than religious parents is whether to tell children *anything* that is based on folk tales, myths, or legends. Santa Claus, the Easter bunny, and the tooth fairy are only a few examples of fictional characters society presents to children as being real...but just until kids grow up. Some atheists question their children on their beliefs about Santa Claus. Eventually, when the children are unable to cite any evidence that Santa exists, they understand that he is a myth people like to believe even though he is not real. These children are taught from an early age to think critically about what society tells them. It is not all right to believe just for the sake of believing.

But is full disclosure really necessary, especially when children are very young? To prevent kids from enjoying Santa Claus, while their young classmates enjoy the excitement of flying reindeer and gifts under a tree, seems almost cruel. My parents did me no harm by telling me the tooth fairy gave me money for the teeth I lost, or that Santa Claus gave me presents. I discovered the truth at some point, and I even played along with the ruse for my younger sister's sake—so why not allow my own kids to grow up with those traditions as well? As I said earlier, atheists are not monolithic in how they approach such issues.

## Religious Expression in Public Life

Because atheist children are in the minority, they face challenges in certain social situations and in school settings. It's difficult for anyone, much less a child, to be singled out for going against the majority. For atheists, refusing to stand and recite the Pledge of Allegiance (which includes the words *under God*) is certainly within their rights, but I would not want my child to feel ostracized from fellow students simply for being true to his atheist beliefs. Even if a child stays seated or chooses to leave the room and stand in the hallway during the reciting of the pledge, he or she is still being singled out on the basis of his or her beliefs.

And it is not just school children who are affected. I plan to be a teacher, but the thought of *not* reciting the Pledge of Allegiance in the classroom gives me pause. I think my approach will be to stand up for the pledge but not recite it. Even making such a compromise makes me wonder if students might complain. Will I be labeled unpatriotic? Could staying faithful to my convictions endanger my job security as a teacher? Would I be tempted to compromise my beliefs just to protect my job, and thus become a hypocrite?

That is, of course, if I even get hired in the first place. I have rewritten my résumé to delete references to my involvement in secular student organizations. This is unfortunate since many of my accomplishments and leadership roles, as well as the people I would like to list as references, come from the nonreligious world. I know if I said I volunteered with my local church, though, there would be no problem. In fact, it might even help me get a job.

## The Question of Death

The most difficult issue for me to deal with when I first became an atheist was death. My grandmother on my mother's side died while I was in high school. I watched my mother and her sisters grieve, and I saw my grandfather go through deep sorrow and withdrawal from daily activities. While he's now able to continue with his life, he had a hard time adjusting to taking care of himself in areas where he had depended on his wife for so long.

How do atheists deal with death, especially when we believe we become nothing more than worm food? Since we don't believe we are headed to a spiritual world, atheists use their view of death to make the end of life meaningful. Many atheists are organ donors—I personally wish organ donation was the default setting on drivers' licenses, with the option to opt out only if you *don't* want to donate your organs. And when organ donation is not an option (which often is the case when a person is elderly), many atheists arrange to donate their bodies to science. Medical students across the country, not to mention their future patients, benefit from this. Being of use even after we die is the ultimate way to help someone else.

I should mention that an atheist's views on death and the lack of an afterlife do not imply atheists are insensitive to death and to those who grieve.

Especially when a relative or close friend has died, I keep my views to myself and let others deal with death according to their beliefs. When my grandmother died, I didn't dare tell my mom I didn't believe Grandma was in heaven. I let the religious processions go on, and I watched the body be cremated (which is a common tradition in Jain culture).

Instead of wondering what happens after death, atheists focus on making the most of *this* life. Therefore, as difficult as it is to do at the funeral of a friend or family member, the focus for atheists is on the great life the deceased person lived on Earth. In that sense, funerals become celebrations of life. While atheists do not believe a spirit still exists, they gain comfort by the fact that the life of the departed lives on in future generations' memories.

In this way, there is an afterlife. Not in a literal or a spiritual sense but in the sense that our legacy lives on after we depart. By donating our bodies and leaving our loved ones with fond memories, we are leaving a part of us for future generations.

## *Minority Status*

It is assumed in America that people believe in God. So where does that leave those of us who don't believe? On television, it's rare to flip through the channels without seeing a televangelist and even rarer to see atheists represented on television, even in a scripted sitcom. In local newspapers, religions of all varieties are showcased (often on the "Religion" pages), yet articles on atheism are rarely published. And I get upset when any nonreligious person, including me, is labeled in the media as an "avowed atheist." The media never refer to an "avowed Jew" or an "avowed Christian." The phrase implies that atheists feel shame and wouldn't have admitted they were nonreligious if they had a choice.

And think about being a nonreligious person and hoping to win a majority of the popular vote in an election. It would be political suicide for a candidate to declare himself or herself an atheist. It doesn't seem to matter to the voters what a candidate's specific religious views are. As long as a candidate has some faith, it's *always* better than having no faith.

This bias is fed by the way the media portray atheists. It's common to hear critics of atheism quoted as saying all atheists are out to destroy religion. While there are popular secular writers who would prefer a religionless world, most atheists I've met would at least be more tolerant of religion if it had no government sponsorship.

When the media bother to notice us at all, the news items almost always relate to stories about lawsuits, such as attempts to take the phrase *under God* out of the Pledge of Allegiance or to remove a nativity scene from public property. Opponents of these efforts would lead you to believe that atheists raise these issues to attack religion, but that's not true. Our real motivation is to respect constitutional guarantees against the governmental establishment of a particular religion. If atheists truly sought to remove religion from public life, I would imagine we would fight to change the line in the Pledge of Allegiance to, "One nation, under *no* God, indivisible." But, of course, this is not the case.

## The Meaning of Life

We can't talk about the beliefs of atheists without addressing the most fundamental question there is: what is the meaning of life? Again, this lacks a simple answer, but atheists have a straight response: we believe that all people choose the meaning in their lives. Some atheists bring meaning by providing for their families. Others dedicate their lives to important causes. Atheists are highly motivated to achieve more in the present life because we believe this is the only life we have.

Maybe that explanation doesn't satisfy you, and you're still wondering what atheists believe the *ultimate* purpose of life is. Well, I'm not sure it's a question anyone can answer.

## AN ATHEIST GOES TO CHURCH

Even if you disagree with my beliefs, understanding my views will help you see why I react in certain ways—and why I am perplexed by certain things—in a church setting. In the next four chapters I'll describe the churches I have visited, and I'll tell you what I felt, experienced, and observed when I was there. I found much that is of value, and I have tried to take those ideas and integrate them into my life.

As I visited each church, I asked myself, *Does Christian faith answer the big questions of life in a more satisfactory way than nonsupernatural explanations do?* I looked for the answer to that question on Saturday nights and Sunday mornings for several months as I sat in fifteen different worship services.

As you join me in a great variety of church settings, you'll have an opportunity to look at Christian worship, teaching, and preaching the way I do. I've learned a lot from going to church. Now you will have a chance to see things in a new light by hearing the Christian message again—this time as it sounds to an atheist.

# The View from a Smaller Pew

*Smaller Does Not Always Mean Closer*

When I was doing the research for this book, I sometimes attended multiple services—at different churches—on the same day. I think I can say with confidence that I was attending church more often than most of the people reading this book, unless you actually work for a church.

In my case I was attending churches of different denominations, with different styles of worship and a variety of approaches to preaching. Being an atheist, I would enter a new church never quite knowing what to expect. Often, the surprises were positive, such as the time the pastor of a very large church walked out into the audience as he preached his sermon, speaking to specific individuals as well as the entire congregation. Other times I was thrown off by confusing rituals. And always, no matter what type of church I was in, I found things that appealed to me and other things that left me cold. I imagine the same type of thing happens to you when you try out a new church.

After visiting fifteen churches in four states—including urban areas, suburbs, and small towns—I realized I needed to organize my findings. In chapter 9 I will summarize the general patterns and trends I observed in the churches I visited. And in the next four chapters, I'll present my critiques of each church. As a way to organize the critiques, I have divided them roughly according to the size of the churches I visited. In this chapter, I'll look at four services that attracted a relatively small crowd. In the next chapter I'll critique midsized congregations, then large churches (in chapter 7), and finally three megachurches (in chapter 8).

No critique is ever objective, and mine are no exception. But their subjectivity is a strength. Any visitor to your church will make subjective judgments, so the tone of my critiques is in keeping with the type of assessment that is made by anyone who visits your church, whether they agree with what you believe or not. Visitors come away with things they appreciate and enjoy, and also things they find confusing and even troubling. Again, my critiques are no exception. The purpose of my church visits was not to look only for things I agreed with or that impressed me positively. I was looking for both sides of the equation—the good and the bad. And, sometimes, the indifferent.

So much for the preamble. Let's go to church.

## LaSalle Street Church, Chicago, Illinois

I began doing church research in Chicago, where I was living at the time I started this experiment. I visited several congregations in the city and surrounding suburbs, and one of the smallest services was held at LaSalle Street Church near downtown.

My trip to LaSalle Street Church began ominously enough: in order to get to the available on-street parking, I had to drive past Locust Street. Fortunately, Moses was nowhere to be seen, and there were no signs of an insect plague in the neighborhood. I had no idea what to expect inside, but had I envisioned a fire-and-brimstone service, I would have been dead wrong.

Normally, the church meets in a larger sanctuary, but since that area was undergoing renovations, we met in Fellowship Hall, a community center that served as a makeshift gathering space. I took a seat near the back of a room filled with several rows of chairs arranged in a semicircle. In the front of the room hung a bed sheet with a picture of a cross on it. The sheet was draped from the low ceiling, and a podium stood in front of it. The backdrop was so straightforward in its simplicity that I felt almost as if I were about to watch a grade-school play. Still, it was appealing.

The seats around me filled quickly, and I was surprised to see a wide age range represented. Many middle-school-age and high-school-age students were among the first to find seats. These kids appeared to have come by themselves! This differed from other churches I visited, where children were almost always accompanied by their parents.

I was prepared for the initial hymns and prayers, since they were a part of the ritual at many of the churches I had already visited. After the first few songs, and after standing and sitting repeatedly, we read some lines from Psalm 33 together. There was no discussion of the verses, so I wasn't sure of the purpose behind reading the passage—perhaps to generate some audience participation, since the men and women were told to read alternating lines. Could that be it?

When the sermon began, I was excited to see a female pastor! I had seen only males on stage at the churches I'd visited up to this point, with the exception of one guest speaker. Perhaps I was about to experience a new type of sermon. Pastor Laura was dressed in comfortable clothes, a suit top with a hemp skirt, and spoke with a pleasing Southern accent. We had just finished reading Colossians 1:9–14, and Pastor Laura referred back to the verses as she mentioned she would talk about being rescued by God. She told a personal story of when she had felt rescued, interjecting side comments and jokes that the audience enjoyed. When she was finishing her story, she told how she felt when she was finally saved, explaining what she was going through and what it meant for her. Everyone's eyes were glued to her.

The rest of her sermon, while referring back to the relevant Bible verses, also contained references to pop culture and global politics. It was a way to remind us that the verses contained special meaning, given the troubled times we live in. Pastor Laura made sure we knew there was a tie between what we heard in church and what we would be challenged by in the coming week outside of church.

Before she ended the sermon, she told us she had just returned from a large conference for pastors at Willow Creek Community Church, a mega-church I discuss in chapter 8. As she described her visit, she talked about entering the Willow Creek campus and the sense of awe she felt as she drove onto the grounds. I had to laugh, because I had felt those same emotions when I had gone there a few weeks earlier. She related stories she had heard from Willow Creek's pastor, Bill Hybels, and again, she pressed home the point that it was *our* responsibility to take Christian teachings and use them to help others, or at least contribute to the church to enable it to take on that task.

Pastor Laura repeated a story she heard at the conference, about how money raised by one church bought enough food to feed a large village. It was a powerful message: just fifty dollars donated as an offering can keep an entire family of four alive in Africa for about a month. I could feel her passion, and I wasn't alone in that. Still, I wasn't sure if she meant to say these efforts were possible because the people donating money were Christians, or merely because they were generous. Even if it was God who motivated them to use their money to help others, it was the donors' decisions that made the charitable work possible. Was she minimizing the power of human kindness? I couldn't tell.

To conclude the morning, Pastor Laura reiterated that being rescued was a powerful moment in anyone's life. Before her sermon began, she had asked some people to participate in an interesting exercise. She had given them each a sheet of paper and asked them to write on one side what they felt before they were rescued by Christ, and on the other, what they felt like afterward. At the end of the sermon, she stepped aside so those people could, one by one, hold out their pieces of paper to show what they were like before, and then flip the paper over to show the change that came about after they were rescued. It was different from anything I had seen at other churches. In fact, this sort of peer teaching was a method I hadn't seen utilized since I had visited a very small house church during my initial research after the eBay auction.

Some of the members wrote that they went from fear to security, dark to light, apathetic to engaged, lonely to befriended, nobody to somebody. And one person, humorously enough, went from blind to near-sighted. Since I was still in the "before" aspect of this exercise, I asked myself if I shared any of these feelings. I rarely feel lonely or apathetic. In fact, atheism has given me more confidence in myself and more passion to help others than I experienced when I was active in the Jain religion.

Reflecting on my life in light of the church members' responses, I had to wonder: was being down, or lonely, or desperate a prerequisite to finding God? Did these people think others who had not yet found Christ were lost, scared, or miserable? Did I have to go through some sort of trauma or crisis before I would find anything of ultimate meaning? Pastor Laura's personal stories of being rescued had been humorous and uplifting. I had expected the others' stories to be similar to that—optimistic, revealing a good life that was made even better. After hearing their stories of before and after, I was upset and somewhat angry. When the people shared their words describing personal change, their representations of being "lost" seemed to include the whole range of people who had not accepted the divinity of Christ. Maybe religion had helped the people who spoke, but I wasn't "lost" in the sense of being miserable, desperate, or without hope.

Yes, I'm an atheist—which means I have no faith in a God, gods, or the supernatural. But I am surrounded by loving people whom I can talk to if I get depressed. I know I can't always control what happens around me, but I can try to react to the unexpected in a positive way. I also know there are questions I just can't answer, such as why the universe exists. For many, religion provides answers to un-answerable questions. But religious "answers" to my unanswerable questions don't satisfy my need for a logical explanation.

While I hadn't been asked to participate in the before-and-after exercise at LaSalle Street Church, I did think about what I would have written when I was in the process of becoming an atheist. Before: Questioning. After: Satisfied, but still questioning.

## EVANGELICAL FREE CHURCH, DEKALB, ILLINOIS

On a different Sunday I drove more than an hour west of Chicago to visit three churches in DeKalb, Illinois. I had never been to DeKalb before; my familiarity with the town was limited to the fact that Northern Illinois University is located there...and Cindy Crawford was born and raised there. But on the summer day when I visited, the university had only a fraction of its student body on campus, and Cindy was nowhere to be seen.

As I approached DeKalb, I was driving on a long stretch of highway that extended in a straight line as far as I could see. At one point I was one of only four motorists on the road, which never happened any morning in Chicago. The miles of cornfields confirmed I was headed to a rural area. While DeKalb is growing in population, it is much smaller than any of the other towns where I have attended church.

I entered the Evangelical Free Church of Sycamore-DeKalb for the 8:30 a.m. service. *What is this church's name all about?* I wondered. *Maybe it's free of evangelicals? Or does it mean no one has to give an offering?* I was directed into the largest room in the church and took a seat toward the back. A one-man technical team was positioned to my right, and a video-projection screen was suspended above the stage (every church seems to have one, regardless of its size). For a room that could seat a couple hundred people at most, I was surprised to see a setup for a full band onstage. Drums, guitars, and several microphones were propped up, ready for use.

When the band started playing, it was just after the 8:30 start time, but there were fewer than forty people in the church. But by the time the band had finished singing and the pastor got up on stage, the crowd had more than doubled in size. I noticed families with young children walking in without any visible indications of guilt. I wouldn't think the people at this church were purposely rude, so they must have had a good reason for showing up late. Was the music so unimportant to them that they decided to come only for the "main event"? If that's the case, is church like a movie theater where you can walk in after the previews and no one thinks anything of it? I've always thought the previews are vital to the movie experience, though, just as I would assume that singing is important to a church service. Furthermore, in a small community church such as this one, I imagine people would know one another better than at a larger church. The people in the congregation, therefore, might know the people on stage who were singing and would surely respect them enough to show up on time. I didn't see that respect being shown, though.

Before the sermon began, announcements were made. A ladies' craft night was scheduled for later in the week, one person mentioned. There would also be a women's prayer group on Wednesday and a men's prayer group on Friday. That sounded odd to me. I had heard of youth Bible studies and adult worship services, and I understand there are good reasons for groups to be separated according to age. But the separation of men from women was a new concept to me. Atheist communities haven't separated the sexes at any meetings I've attended. What was so different about prayer meetings that men and women couldn't pray together?

Later on, I had a chance to ask the pastor why men and women needed to be separated for prayer. Pastor Brad said such an arrangement gave both men and women a chance for "more intimate sharing" of concerns. For example, women could talk about upcoming surgeries they might feel uncomfortable sharing if men were present. I assume the same reasoning applied to men. However, for something as solemn as a prayer meeting, would the potential for awkwardness really present that much of a deterrent? It didn't make sense to me that someone would request prayer from only half the adults in the congregation. While I don't believe prayer has a direct effect on someone's health, wouldn't Christians want *more* people praying for them, rather than dividing their support in half by excluding an entire gender?

On the Sunday I visited his church, Pastor Brad spoke on the topic of contentment. His main point was that we should be happy with what we have. As I listened, I realized I am often motivated by *not* being satisfied. I don't mean I'm motivated to obtain more material goods. Rather, I'm motivated to achieve goals. If we're always content with where we are and what we have, there would be no need to try to improve ourselves. But in his sermon, I didn't hear any encouragement to work toward goals or to improve ourselves.

To illustrate his point, Pastor Brad began by telling a story about a man who kept wanting more and more until finally he realized he had everything he wanted all along. Later he told a story about Aleksandr Solzhenitsyn, the Russian author who won the Nobel Prize in Literature. While in prison, Solzhenitsyn rejected Marxism and began a journey toward Christian faith. The theme of Pastor Brad's sermon was Be Satisfied with Your Life, so I wasn't sure why he used Solzhenitsyn's story, since the author's life changed so dramatically. I didn't notice this at first. Initially, I was captivated by the story. When I reflected on it later, however, I began to think it didn't fit with the morning's theme.

Pastor Brad also denounced a segment of Christian television he characterized as "pop psychology wrapped in Bible verses" and presented by people telling us to not be content. We need to be content with where we are in life, Pastor Brad repeated. I felt like he was missing the point. Those "pop psychology" pastors tell us to do more with our lives and to strive for more. It isn't about being greedy; it's about getting the most out of life. In my mind, contentment is not a virtue if it leads to apathy, detachment, or lack of involvement in the world.

As the message went on, I found I wasn't enjoying myself in the same way

I had in other churches. And it wasn't because I preferred sermons that were sugarcoated. Instead, I was put off by the lack of humor and the formality of Pastor Brad's presentation. After visiting other churches, I had grown to appreciate certain elements of preaching that hold the audience's attention. Other pastors made humor the centerpiece of their sermons, while staying focused on the themes of their messages. They told us what would happen if we followed their advice. They stepped away from the podiums and spoke to the congregations as if everyone knew one another well. Those qualities made those pastors more compelling and even more likable, even as they conveyed messages not that different from the one I was hearing on this morning. At the Evangelical Free Church, many people in the audience weren't laughing. They seemed to be as uncomfortable as I was.

The pastor set a tone of formality by wearing a white shirt, red tie, blue blazer, and khaki pants. Anyone who showed up in jeans would have felt very out of place. This isn't to say it's bad for people to wear dressy clothing to church. But the pastor's formality, along with his very serious sermon, made the service feel like a dull college lecture.

When I visit a church, I bring along a pen and a spiral notebook. I take a lot of notes, not just on the sermon but on the setting and the atmosphere, the look of the sanctuary or auditorium, the mood of the congregation, and a lot of other things. I did the same at this church, but an hour into it I began to drift off. And here's the interesting thing: I wasn't alone. As I looked around, I saw many people looking at their programs or at other families. Often, they'd look at their watches. They clearly weren't focused on the message. The children who had not gone to the Sunday-school class weren't that different, spending the morning coloring their Children's Worship Bulletins.

As I studied the congregation, I noticed something I hadn't expected at a church in a smaller community. Most of the families chose to sit by themselves with empty seats surrounding them. The next closest family would be several seats away, or sitting in a different row. Where was the close bond I expected to find in a rural town? I grew up in a religious family that was part of a tight-knit religious community. When our group got together for worship and teaching, we kids would make sure we sat next to each other. The adults would say hello to their friends before taking seats among them. (And if a prayer had started, they would at least acknowledge their friends silently.) Everyone looked forward to seeing one another at these gatherings. I expected no less at a small church located in a small town. But I didn't notice a special bond connecting these families. Even the children, whom I expected to rush to sit next to one another, sat with their own families.

At other churches I had attended, the services ended with more songs, announcements to remind the congregation of upcoming events, or blessings being pronounced. This morning, however, the pastor talked and talked and then suddenly said, "Amen." Before I knew it, everyone was getting up and walking out. That was it? It wasn't even a collective amen. There was not even an, "Okay, you can go now," or, "There are refreshments in the lobby." It was very abrupt. By that point, I was ready to join the others who were racing out the front door to their cars.

## WESTMINSTER PRESBYTERIAN CHURCH, DEKALB, ILLINOIS

The next stop on my DeKalb, Illinois, road trip was Westminster Presbyterian Church, only a couple of miles from the Evangelical Free Church. I arrived just as the service was about to begin. When I stepped into the meeting hall, I noticed for the first time in the months I'd been going to church services that there were no separate seats. I had to sit in an actual pew! Attached to the back of the pew in front of me was a large wooden pocket containing two Bibles, two hymnbooks, paper that people could use for writing prayer requests, and information about ministries the church offered.

The atmosphere was somber. The stained-glass windows around the room didn't create a picture; they were just small, amorphous shapes. There was an organ in the front. No drummer this time. I didn't even bother looking for electric guitars.

People began to file into the pews shortly after I took my seat and just before the first hymn was sung. Compared to the church I had visited earlier that morning, this one was more crowded, and the average age had skyrocketed. A few children were present, but most in the congregation had gray hair. They were very cordial to one another and chose seats close to one another. For some reason, it seemed as if the entire room was full…except for a ten-seat perimeter around where I was sitting. I didn't know if it was because I was sitting with a notebook, writing, or because I was an unfamiliar brown person in a sea of whiteness, but only when the other areas became crowded did anyone choose a seat closer to me.

As I filled out a "friendship book" with my name and contact information, the pastor came in wearing a robe with a green sash around his neck. I looked at my program to see what he was going to speak on but couldn't find any mention of a sermon. The first page of the program listed the prayers everyone would recite, followed by a hymn, then a scripted "call to worship" between a leader and the churchgoers, then another hymn, then a call to confession, a poem, more scripted text between a leader and us, more singing, a performance by a children's choir, another prayer, and finally, at the bottom of the second page, I saw one line that mentioned a sermon.

Compared to the songs sung at other churches I had visited, Westminster Presbyterian used hymns that were more solemn and old-fashioned. But other than that, they weren't much different from songs I had heard in other churches. When it came time for the scripted readings, though, I had a hard time understanding the point behind them.

The leader would say, "Our help is in the name of the Lord."

We would respond, "Who made heaven and earth."

The leader would say, "Those who wait upon the Lord shall renew their strength."

We would respond, "They shall mount up with wings as eagles."

And so on.

It was all written there for us, but what was the purpose? To get us more involved? If it was meant to energize us about God, you would never have guessed from the lackluster responses given by the congregation. If it was meant to be a prayer, it gave no evidence of being heartfelt. If it was just a ritual, I didn't see the point. I recalled some of the Jain rituals that never made sense to me when I was growing up. There were times I was supposed to kneel when I prayed, but only on my right knee; there were certain words I was supposed to say when I walked into the temple; there was even a specific way I was supposed to say certain mantras—and repeat them exactly one hundred eight times. Even if there were reasons behind the rituals, the reasons were never apparent and rarely satisfied my curiosity. I felt the same way this morning in church.

After the children's choir finished singing, I saw that the program mentioned there would be an Old Testament "lesson" (in this case, 2 Samuel 7:1–7), a response (Psalm 89), and a New Testament "lesson" (Ephesians 2:11–22 and Mark 6:30–34, 53–56). When we arrived at that point in the service, the Bible verses were read out loud by a leader, and then we sang another hymn.

I had to wonder, *What happened to the lesson?* There was no teaching or explanation, just the various Bible readings. Perhaps the word *lesson* was code for scripted Bible readings, but I certainly didn't learn anything from them.

The pastor finally took his place on the stage and began to speak. Pastor Blake made quick references to the Bible passages, though his voice was not helping me stay awake. He spoke in a monotone, with a steady volume and low energy level the entire time. In all, there was only a five-minute sermon before he called to the stage anyone who wanted to be baptized. A young couple joined him. They repeated an Affirmation of Faith, and the man had water put on his head. (I assumed the woman had already been baptized and had brought along her new husband to do the same, but I didn't know for certain.)

The program then called for the ordination of elders and deacons. I took these to be titles of respect that would be reserved for only a handful of people. In fact, just three people were ordained that morning. The pastor then called for those who already held the titles to come grasp the hands or shoulders of the newcomers. I expected another one or two people to go up to the stage, but instead nearly *half the audience* went up. I was missing out on something. Either it didn't take much to earn the title of elder or deacon, or everyone had been coming to this church for a very long time.

More prayers were said. There was another offering. And a few hymns later, we ended the service. The number of times I stood up and sat back down made it feel like I had just finished a long workout.

I admit I'm far from knowledgeable about the traditions and beliefs of a Presbyterian church. But I can say I felt no connection to this church. Had I come more often, I suspect I could become close to the members, but the rituals and scripted prayers turned me off. When a newcomer enters a place of worship and is unfamiliar with the rituals, it can make him or her uncomfortable. What would happen, for instance, if I didn't kneel at the right time, or if I didn't know to stand during certain prayers, or if I failed to repeat the words we were given? Well...nothing. Except I'd feel awkward and out of place. Rituals happen largely without thought. You just do them without thinking about it. I prefer activity that makes you think, which is why I appreciated sermons that left me rethinking my own life.

Aside from being made to feel you don't belong, I also don't see the religious reason for rituals. If I wanted to feel close to God, the prayers would have to come from within, tailored to my own struggles, hopes, and gratitude. A scripted prayer took away from all that.

Once we were finished, I had only a couple of minutes before the next church service was to begin, so I took off for First Lutheran Church, hoping I would find a stronger connection there.

## FIRST LUTHERAN CHURCH, DeKALB, ILLINOIS

The 11:15 a.m. service at First Lutheran Church was not a traditional service (that had occurred earlier in the day). This was to be an informal praise service, which made me wonder if there would be a lot of singing without a full-fledged sermon. Actually, that wasn't too far off. When I entered, albeit a few minutes late, I heard the words to a familiar song. The program I was handed said this song was called "Open the Eyes of My Heart." I had to look through my program from the Evangelical Free Church I'd attended earlier that morning. My hunch was right; I had heard this song already. Was that a coincidence, or was it just a popular song?

The Lutheran service took place in the church's atrium. There were only four rows of seats set up, and not too many people filling them. A number of high-school students were present, and I figured most of the adults in attendance were their parents.

A couple more songs were sung before the pastor, a woman, began reading the scripture. Again, there wasn't a discussion. It was simply a reading. And these words also sounded strangely familiar. I glanced at the program. *Ephesians 2:11–22 and Mark 6:30–34, 53–56.* It was the same material I had heard less than an hour earlier at the Presbyterian church. What was going on in DeKalb? Did all the churches have some schedule that determined which verses should be read on which day?

It turns out they did. I spoke to Pastor Marilyn after my visit, and she told me her church uses the Revised Common Lectionary,[1] a collection of Bible verses to be read on certain weeks. These verses are used in a three-year cycle. I asked Pastor Marilyn if the three-year cycle was in place so all the verses in the Bible could be read over that time period. No, the pastor responded. Only certain books were used. The Gospels and Psalms were well represented. "What about Leviticus?" I asked. (Atheists often point to passages in Leviticus as evidence that the Bible includes horrible acts of violence.) Pastor Marilyn said it wasn't included in the readings. And the song I heard when I walked in? Was that also specified in advance or was that just a coincidence? The pastor laughed as she said it was just a popular song.

After the Bible reading, Pastor Marilyn mentioned that a number of the teenagers had attended a conference in Texas and that the students wanted to thank the supporters who made the trip possible. The conference was called the Evangelical Lutheran Church in America (ELCA) Youth Gathering, and each student explained how he or she grew closer to God through the experience. The pictures that played on a screen in the background showed the inside of the Alamodome, packed with teenagers and adult chaperones.

The students shared that fifteen thousand youth had participated in this event. Fifteen thousand? *Wow.* I was jealous. Most atheist conventions I had attended attracted several dozen college students—nowhere close to hundreds or thousands. It wasn't that there are so few of us, but it was difficult to get the funding to bring everyone to one centralized location. Even so, those conferences left us students excited and ready to be more active in our local groups. As the Lutheran kids talked about the event they had attended, I was amazed by how life-changing the experience was for so many of them. Many students noted this was the first time they had met such a large gathering of people who shared the same beliefs they did. They came back energized about the church and eager to share their faith with others.

As I listened, I could imagine certain atheists saying that a church conference is a way to brainwash youth into thinking that just because something is fun, it must be valid. To that end, I didn't hear the students mention any sessions where they were taught to think critically about their faith. Then again, I'm not sure I would expect a session like that at a religious conference.

The conference presented the kids with a chance to interact with other teenagers and have a good time. Theology may have been taught, but it wasn't the focal point for most of the students who spoke about it. From that standpoint, I'm glad they had a good time. I do think it would be beneficial for the students to learn what non-Christians think and how to interact with them. To teach this at a conference of this size might be the best way to create a positive change for the future.

Interestingly enough, the students' descriptions of their experiences were not far from those I've heard from students who have attended secular conferences. Among atheist college students, when they have a chance to speak to other students who often share similar "coming out" stories and experiences, it's a powerful step in affirming one's nonbelief in God. For the Lutheran students, many had never been around a group of like-minded people and were excited to bring back the new ideas and activities to First Lutheran Church.

After the students spoke, Pastor Marilyn returned to the podium to share her message, which was the closest we came to discussing the Bible passages. Again, it didn't last very long. Then more hymns were sung, the offering plate was passed, and the Lord's Prayer was recited.

If this informal gathering was any indication of the more formal service that had been held at First Lutheran earlier that morning, I was disappointed I had missed the other service. It would have been interesting to hear Pastor Marilyn give a more complete sermon, as well as give me a chance to compare the effect of a formal service on those who attended. Did the closeness I observed among those who attended the informal service grow out of the informality, or would I have noticed a similar degree of closeness at the formal service?

On other weekends I attended churches larger than the ones in DeKalb—but still not megachurch huge—in Chicago, Houston, and Colorado Springs. They shared some similarities with the churches I have described in this chapter, and a lot of differences, which I came to expect. Often when I visited a different church, my preconceived notions of church were reinforced. However, the midsized churches I attended forced me to set many of those notions aside. I'll report on the midsized churches in the next chapter.

# The View from a Midsized Pew

## On Sunday Morning, Size Makes a Difference

After reporting in the last chapter on my visits to small churches, it's time to comment on some midsized churches. But first, let me make a necessary clarification. In most circles, the churches I critique in this chapter would be considered large churches. They attract a combined weekend attendance that far exceeds the national average, which stands at well below two hundred worshipers.[1] And in the case of Windsor Village United Methodist Church, its membership figures put the church in the "mega" category.

So you might wonder why I'm grouping these churches in the midsized category. Primarily, it's because the feel of the services I attended is midsized. Because these churches have multiple weekend services, and one of the churches has three different campuses, the attendance at one service numbers only in the hundreds. *Only* in the hundreds? Yes, hundreds of worshipers are considered midsized when compared to the thousands in attendance in one auditorium at the megachurches. I mention this because I don't want you to send me e-mails challenging my classification system. I understand that the three churches I describe in this chapter are, in fact, large churches. Let's begin in Colorado, at Calvary Worship Center.

## CALVARY WORSHIP CENTER, COLORADO SPRINGS, COLORADO

In the foothills of the Rocky Mountains, on the west side of Colorado Springs, I visited the early service (of three Sunday services) at Calvary Worship Center. The church seats several hundred people in its main meeting area (a new sanctuary is being built that will double the seating capacity), with an overflow room that seats another seventy-five.

When I walked into the church lobby, the first thing I saw was a map of the world on the wall listing various outreach ministries. The map was divided into three parts labeled Judea, Samaria, and the Ends of the Earth, with each category representing ministry efforts and mission work supported by Calvary Chapel churches. Under the Judea ministries, a statistic was listed indicating a conversion rate of twenty people per one million hours of ministry involvement. I wasn't sure what the baseline statistic was supposed to be, but keeping track of conversions in this way made it seem like the "over 99 billion served" signs at a McDonald's. Why focus on the quantity of conversions and not the quality of the help that is being provided? I'd rather see statistics on how many people's lives have been improved, or even literally saved, by missionaries through the building of homes, the delivery of vaccines, agricultural development, clean-water projects, nutrition programs, and so on. I also wondered if missionaries went back and checked on the people they claimed to help to make sure their efforts were having a long-term impact.

I went into the sanctuary and easily found a good seat. In fact, empty seats were available throughout most of the room. Even several minutes later, after the opening music ended and the latecomers had arrived, the room still had many empty seats. Was the room this empty because it was the early service? Why come to the 8:00 a.m. service when there are two more services afterward, I suppose.

I was relieved to have a clear sight of the stage without having to bend my neck to see around a video camera, as I had done in other churches. Was this a church that didn't feel it necessary to videotape every service? It had been a while since I had seen that happen! But as I looked around a bit more, I saw two camcorders mounted on poles and pointing at the stage.

The band and the singers took the stage to sing the usual songs of praise. The only difference was the band included a jazz trumpeter and a man playing bongos. *That* was an interesting twist. No matter. The band was impressive, and their passion seemed to enliven the crowd. As I watched the lyrics that were displayed on the large screen in front, though, I noticed a line that bothered me. The congregation was singing, "One day every tongue will confess You are God." (This is a paraphrase of a Bible passage, Philippians 2:10–11.) Is that a wish, or is it a fact? Either way, it frightens me. I haven't confessed anyone is God, so where does that leave me? What it is about my worldview that is so threatening?

I imagined what might happen if the people at Calvary Worship Center were present at the temple of another religion and heard people singing about a different deity they felt would one day be praised by everyone. Wouldn't these people singing to the Christian God be upset by that? But I don't think anyone was thinking along those lines. They sang along and enjoyed the music.

Before the pastor got on stage, a man came up to talk about his mission work in the Middle East and North Africa. He described his conversion to Christianity, saying Jesus had appeared to him and showed him His wounded hand, and as a result he was able to say, "Now I believe!" As I listened, I couldn't help but think that his personal experience did not constitute proof of anything.

I started to think of other explanations for his vision of Jesus. Perhaps it was nothing more than a vivid dream, or even wishful thinking. Plus, his story sounded a lot like the Doubting Thomas story from the Bible. Maybe years earlier he had somehow heard about Doubting Thomas but had forgotten the story. Later, he may have recalled parts of the story and somehow thought it happened to him. But this was just my mind wandering. I had no way of knowing the details of the man's story, and I was in no position to present alternative theories that might explain his vision. He asked at the end of his speech if everyone believed his story. "Yes!" the audience replied. I remained silent.

This church, with a multiethnic congregation but still predominantly white, is led by a black pastor. As Pastor Al took the stage, he called out, "How many believe the Lord is our ruler? Raise your hands high!" Was this a question that needed to be asked in church? But then I wondered if people who attend church regularly, when they hear such a question, simply raise their hands due to peer pressure. Being an atheist, I didn't care who was looking at the hands I kept at my side.

Pastor Al has a booming voice, and even though this was an early-morning service, the people were wide awake, listening to everything he said. It was hard to ignore him; the microphone was unnecessary. He spent the morning talking about overcoming mediocrity. He told us the Holy Spirit was someone who would lift us up when we were down. *Isn't that one reason we have human friends?* I wondered.

Besides the obvious passion and conviction he had for what he was saying, Pastor Al was funny, and he had a way of mentioning specific examples from the Bible and popular culture but also putting those examples in a larger context. He cited Matthew 14:31 (the verse in which Jesus asks Peter why he has so little faith about being able to walk on water). Some atheists might take Jesus' words here to seem harsh and impatient. However, Pastor Al explained that this was not a rebuke; Jesus was being compassionate. After giving several other examples of why we needed to have faith, he explained that we have settled for mediocrity in our lives when Jesus has so much more prepared for us. They were powerful words for those sitting around me.

I appreciated his desire to help his audience rise above mediocrity. But I was thrown off by some of the statements he made. For example, he stated that offering young people condoms is an example of "giving in" to a lower standard and added that our lives are consumed by demonic lies. Satan told us we were losers—a lie we needed to ignore. Pastor Al also talked about how we were wandering around lost because we haven't done what Jesus wants.

Ideologically, I disagreed with him. I certainly wasn't lost or following the lies of Satan, and I could think of several benefits of making condoms available to young people. Given the high percentage of teenagers and college students who engage in sex, why not do something to help reduce the spread of STDs and unwanted pregnancies, in addition to teaching the benefits of abstinence?

I would have appreciated it if Pastor Al had given specific reasons for his opposition to condom distribution. It seems that pastors in general just assume everyone in the audience already agrees with them. They don't often provide reasons or explanations to back up what they say. They might use a statistic or an example to make a point, but almost always without citing a source. It's as if they think we should believe them simply because a pastor is saying it.

An assertion that comes up again and again in churches is the idea that non-Christians are lost. I really would like to hear an explanation to back up that statement. I don't feel lost; in fact, I've felt found ever since I became an atheist. So I'd like to hear a pastor tell me why he's convinced I am lost.

When Pastor Al's sermon was nearing its end, I was ready to hear a powerful closing, something that would send me off with a sense of urgency and the feeling that I needed to overcome mediocrity in my life. What would he say to spark something within me?

"You're dismissed," said Pastor Al.

## MARS HILL BAPTIST CHURCH, CHICAGO, ILLINOIS

Mars Hill Baptist Church is an African American congregation on the west side of Chicago. The church first opened in 1963, and it has a straightforward mission statement. Mars Hill Baptist "exists to turn the unchurched into fully devoted followers of Christ." It was Sunday morning, and I was in the right building, so what was I in for this morning? Was I about to become a devoted follower of Christ?

When I walked in, the greeters were excited to see me. I wondered if the attention I was receiving had to do with my skin color. Did I stand out because I wasn't black? Or was it because I was young? Nope. I flattered myself too much. The greeters treated everyone the same way as they welcomed the people behind me.

The main room of the church was relatively small compared to others I had visited. There were four sections of pews stretching to the back of the room and a large aisle down the center, perfect for a wedding ceremony.

As I read the program, I grew excited about the sermon topic: Sometimes I Have My Doubts About God. I couldn't wait to hear what the pastor had to say on the topic.

The seats filled up as the starting time approached, and I saw only one person who was undoubtedly not African American. I was curious about what drew her here. One of my friends from high school, a white girl, always attended a black church with her family. She said the reason was that the pastor was so amazing. I didn't know if the woman I noticed this morning had a similar reason for attending this church or whether she was drawn there by friends. (Later, after I heard Pastor Clarence speak, I suspected his sermons had a role to play.)

While the number in attendance here was nowhere near that of Reverend James Meeks's huge Salem Baptist Church on Chicago's south side, the choir was just as powerful. It sounded like I was attending the opera. I also enjoyed watching the choir director, who danced around as much as some of the choir members.

When Pastor Clarence first began speaking, the music was still playing, and every now and then the choir would utter shouts of praise. As a result, it was hard for me to understand what he was saying. I'm not sure it mattered initially, though, because his sermon had not yet officially begun. He was injecting some energy into the crowd, and it was working. It was evident that people were excited to be here.

I agreed with the pastor's optimism for the wonderful day we were having, but his words quickly became repetitious.

It's good to be here! *Yes, it is.*

Are you blessed? *Sure.*

I said, it's good to be here! *I agree.*

We are blessed! *Okay.*

Are we blessed? *I answered that already.*

Praise Jesus! *We just did.*

It's good to be here! *Oh boy...*

I wasn't accustomed to this type of audience participation.

When Pastor Clarence finally began his sermon, he made the confession up-front that even *he* has doubts about God sometimes. It was humbling and important to hear that. The people in the audience, having experienced doubt themselves, nodded their heads as he spoke. His ability to step into the minds of those of us in the pews made Pastor Clarence enjoyable to listen to. He spoke about his father, a founder and the original pastor of this church, and how he passed away at a young age. Pastor Clarence noted that it always seemed like the good people were taken away and the evil folk lived. ("Amen," said the crowd.) He said many modern churches leave no room for doubt. ("You said it!" shouted one woman.) The pastor elaborated on these points by walking through the issues that were going through our minds.

Other parts of his sermon included lines such as: "Money don't make you happy…but neither does being poor!" ("Hallelujah!" shouted the crowd); "I feel that God is real, but when my major issues arise, where is He?" ("Amen!"); "I'm here to tell you God is good! If you have doubts, fifty-percent faith, or thirty-percent faith, let Jesus meet you where you are!"

Pastor Clarence told a story from Mark 9:21–23 about a man who brought his sick son to Jesus. The boy's father said to Jesus, "If you can do anything…help us."[2] Jesus responded, " 'If you can'?… Everything is possible for him who believes."[3]

What made the story so effective was that after reading the first lines, the pastor stepped back and told the audience he was going to unpack what just happened. He essentially acted out the lines with the proper emphases so we could understand how Jesus must have felt when he heard the man's questions. It wasn't a lengthy passage, but we were able to get more out of it due to the pastor's interpretations.

In fact, I think Pastor Clarence could have said anything he wanted with the voice, tone, and intensity he was using, and the audience would have cheered and clapped. I enjoyed his sermon, but I still had not found the answer, or *any* answer, to the question of what I should do with my doubts.

The pastor then began the story of Doubting Thomas. At the time I didn't know this story very well (I visited Mars Hill Baptist before Calvary Worship Center). All I could infer was that Thomas doubted Jesus in some way—so I listened carefully. In John 20:25 Thomas said he wouldn't believe in the resurrection of Christ unless he saw and touched Jesus' hands where the nails had been driven in at the crucifixion.

I could see this in my mind, and it seemed like a good idea to me: Thomas demanded proof.

The story continues a week later. Jesus suddenly appeared and told Thomas to touch his hands and his side. Thomas had his proof, and he believed (see John 20:26–28).

It was an interesting story. I'd had the impression that people looked down on Thomas for doubting Jesus. And yet, here he was asking for the same thing I was looking for: evidence. Thomas saw his evidence standing right in front of him. I kept thinking if Jesus did that to me now, I'm sure I'd change my mind, too! So why are atheists so despised for thinking like Thomas did?

Pastor Clarence continued his sermon on doubt, and the only answer I heard about how to overcome my doubts was when he paraphrased the words of the sick boy's father in the earlier story: "I want to believe—help me get there" (see Mark 9:24). That was one answer, I suppose, but it didn't quite do it for me.

Still, Pastor Clarence was a compelling speaker, and his power came from his knowledge of what everyone in the audience was thinking. He knew the challenges and life circumstances of the members of the congregation. He took those thoughts and put them right back out there, and it helped make the connection that brought these people back and, I'm sure, attracted new members every week.

## WINDSOR VILLAGE UNITED METHODIST CHURCH, HOUSTON, TEXAS

Windsor Village United Methodist Church, like Mars Hill Baptist, is an African American church. I attended a service held at one of the church's three locations in Houston. And if you watched either of George W. Bush's inaugurations on television, you have seen the church's senior pastor, Kirbyjon Caldwell. He gave the benediction on both occasions.

The Sunday morning I visited, the pews were packed, and as the choir sang I was sure the music could be heard well outside the walls of the church. The lyrics to the songs were displayed on large screens located high on a wall behind the choir, and when the louder portions were sung, the words were written in all capital letters.

Since this was not the first African American church I had visited, I wondered if some of the things I had experienced at other similar churches would hold true here as well. The church literature mentioned that the senior pastor's wife had the title of "first lady." I had seen this at another African American church and had initially thought it was just arrogance. Now I was learning that the title was not unique to just one church. I suppose it's a way to honor the wife of the senior pastor.

I knew music was a large part of the worship experience in African American churches, so I expected the service to run long. But at Windsor Village, it kept going. And going. It wasn't just the length of the songs that bothered me; the lyrics added to my irritation. The lines and the refrains were repeated so many times I lost count. Why do churches do this? What's the point of so much repetition?

One part of the music I did enjoy was watching one of the church's ministers take the microphone. As the choir sang in the background, he began swaying. Then he began clapping. Then he began jumping. It was intense. The audience followed his actions. The passion remained at a high level for the entire forty-five minutes they sang. In between the songs, there were prayers, a brief video promo for upcoming events, and a welcome to visitors. But those interludes were short. Most of the time was dedicated to singing.

Eventually, the music came to a rest. Before the guest speaker was introduced, we were told that a person had passed away during the week, and that he was now with God. For those who didn't recognize the name, we were also told that this was the person the church had prayed for the previous week, as his health was deteriorating. As more information was given, I reran that dialogue in my head. The congregation had prayed for this man, but he died. The people had prayed he would get better…but he died. How did that work, exactly? And what did it mean?

If the church had prayed for him to get better but it didn't work, something must have gone wrong. Did people not pray hard enough? It was clear the people didn't feel their prayers were useless. But how was it possible to keep praying for other things when it was clear that in this instance prayer hadn't worked?

It seemed that we were being told to thank God when our prayers came true and good things happened, but we also were reminded that it was still God's will if our prayers did not come true. (A similar thing had happened at Willow Creek Community Church in the Chicago suburbs, as you'll see in chapter 8. The speaker that day mentioned the story of Joseph being sold into slavery and later being imprisoned on false charges despite his strong faith.) In my mind, the two assertions are not compatible. Either God listens or He doesn't. Perhaps the prayers fall on deaf ears (or no ears at all, as I thought), and if God's will was going to win out regardless, then praying is a moot point. Why bother praying if it makes no difference in the end?

We were then told about the guest speaker: Pastor Rhenell was a woman who had once attended this church. Now she was a pastor herself, having led other churches in Houston. She spoke about a story told in Matthew 9 where Jesus healed a paralytic man. Jesus forgave the man and told him to get off his mat and go home. And the man did so, much to the surprise of the on-lookers (see verses 6–8). The speaker used this story as a metaphor for the problems we all have. She told us Jesus would forgive us regardless of the problem we faced. No matter what was on our mat (referring metaphorically to the paralyzed man's mat), we needed to get off it, take our mat with us so no one in the future (such as our children) would stumble over our problems, and move on.

She brought along a prop to drive the point home—a long cloth banner. Held up during the sermon by two church members, the banner had written on it different problems we commonly face. These were the problems we were told to get rid of: jealousy, hate, racism, unforgiveness, abortion, pride, pornography, child abuse, and several others. At first, I agreed with the prob-lems enumerated on her list. But I started to get frustrated when I heard her say homosexuality was a problem. (In my view, you are born either hetero-sexual or homosexual, so why consider an innate predisposition to be a prob-lem?) But I put that thought aside when I heard the speaker mention another problem: witchcraft. Really? I didn't know people still took witchcraft seri-ously. Was this pastor like the religious people who want to ban Harry Potter?

I decided to give Pastor Rhenell the benefit of the doubt because she did have a positive message. She pointed out that when we succumb to certain problems, it makes life worse for us. Furthermore, some of these problems stay in a family through multiple generations. We need to ask God for for-giveness and not let anyone else be affected negatively by these issues.

She told stories of people who had been abused and then later abused their own children. As I listened, I recalled stories I had heard of families that were still angry with one another over feuds their ancestors had generations ago. These are problems that need to be stopped before they spread. The more Pastor Rhenell spoke, the more everyone was moved by her message. I knew this because people around me kept encouraging her as she spoke, ask-ing for more, saying "amen" with each sentence.

Toward the end, the speaker asked us to recite the following words to begin the process of forgiveness and to help us "get off the mat" of our prob-lems: "God, I love you more than my car, my home, my family…" Again, I had to stop and give that some thought. I understood the idea of loving God more than anything material. But to love God more than one's *family*? This raised all kinds of questions. Why not ask parents which child they love more?

I couldn't imagine a person prioritizing God before his wife or their chil-dren or their parents, even if everyone in the family believed in the same reli-gion. Faith might be important, but is it so important that if we had to choose between family and faith, someone would tell her family they came in second place? Maybe I read too much into it, because the other people in the church applauded enthusiastically when Pastor Rhenell was finished. A minister took the stage and said it was the best interpretation of that scripture he had ever heard—the audience agreed.

With a few more announcements and songs, the service ended.

In my months of visiting churches, I have attended three African American churches. In general, I have enjoyed the services. It's exciting to see the passion that is expressed. Furthermore, these churches focus on achieving social equality and fixing communities that need help. Churches that are predominantly white don't ignore these issues, of course, but they seem to focus more on personal growth with God.

One reason I notice the African American churches' commitment to meeting physical and social needs is because it's much harder for atheists to argue that religion leads to problems when you see faith guiding people to help the world become better for everyone, regardless of religion or race. To that end, the title of the Windsor Village United Methodist Church Web site is Kingdom Builders, because they want to create on earth what they think they will see in heaven. Their extensive ministries have brought social services, commercial enterprises, health services, educational opportunities, job-skills assistance, and much more to an underserved area in Houston. In addition, the church is the moving force behind the development of a mixed-income and mixed-use master planned community, as well as a private school for children through the eighth grade. And that list includes only a fraction of this church's incredible accomplishments.

Becoming Kingdom Builders is a lofty but worthy goal, and while I may take issue with some of the statements I heard in the sermon, it's obvious there is an impressive amount of good work being done through this church.

Few churches have the resources or the expertise to engineer the far-reaching, community-enhancing work that Windsor Village United Methodist Church is doing. In fact, the church is planning to build a new ministry complex with a sanctuary that will seat sixty-five hundred in a single service. So much for Windsor Village being a midsized church.[4]

Let's move on to some large churches, bearing in mind that the adjective is a relative measure. In Illinois, Colorado, and Texas we'll visit churches that come across as large whether you visit on Saturday night or Sunday morning.

# The View from a Larger Pew

*It's Hard to Beat the Advantages Found in Large Churches*

hurches come in all sizes, but the four I critique in this chapter are unmistakably *large*. From the time you set foot on their campuses, you know you're onto something big.

The one thing that stands out, even to an atheist, is that large churches have the resources available to do impressive things. Also, with just one exception among the large churches I visited, their speakers are topnotch.

As I did my research, I visited so many large churches—some of them among the highest-profile churches in the country—that I'm devoting two chapters to the critiques. For starters, join me for services at four very large churches in three different states.

## SECOND BAPTIST CHURCH, HOUSTON, TEXAS

I don't know whose job it is to name churches, but if you're going to be the second Baptist church in a town, why not come up with a more imaginative name? I would apply the same rule to all Baptist churches (or Methodist, or

Lutheran) that aren't the first ones in their locales. (I spent quite a bit of time on Google typing in "Third Baptist Church," "Fourth Baptist Church," and so forth, wondering how high the numbering might reach. The result was astonishing. Try it yourself.)

Despite its name, Second Baptist Church is no obscure, also-ran church. It serves an incredibly large membership in Houston, with six different church campuses. At a Saturday-night service, I had a chance to listen to Ben Young, an associate pastor and Christian author and son of senior pastor, Dr. Ed Young.

As I entered the building from the church's parking lot, I could hear smooth, jazzy music playing. It was a calm and welcoming sound. As I listened more closely, I realized it was a rendition of a Rob Thomas song, something I'd heard on the radio just days earlier. The church certainly wanted to appeal to young people. I also saw in the church's program that they had a contemporary service for certain churchgoers, perhaps those in their thirties or younger, which begins precisely at 11:11 a.m., a time that holds a superstitious significance for some young people. (They often make a wish when a clock reads 11:11.)

A sign outside the building indicated that tonight's sermon was going to be "Pete's Story," which sounded like a title that would appeal to a younger person as well—"Pete" sounds like a buddy you had in college. This church had several indications of being one I might enjoy.

The building itself is enormous—I've seen community colleges smaller than this church. Inside the building I looked for what I knew to expect in a megachurch: the bookstore, the restaurant, the day-care center. They were all there. The printed program included an insert listing the numerous services provided by the church. One of them was a twenty-four-hour prayer line. That idea intrigued me because I didn't think such a service would be used very often. Do people wake up in the middle of the night and suddenly realize they need an emergency prayer? I wanted to find out what it was all about, so late at night on a Sunday, a few weeks after visiting the church, I called the prayer hotline. I wasn't sure what I was going to say, but it didn't matter. I got the answering machine.

Understand that I was simply checking it out; I wasn't experiencing a crisis. And on other occasions, I'm sure someone is there to help. But let's say I needed a listening ear and someone who would pray for me over the phone. I'm sure that getting an answering machine would be a disappointment to someone in a real crisis who felt prayer might help.

Before the Saturday-night service began, I stepped into the auditorium and took a seat in a pew close to the middle of the seating area. For the first time in my church visits, I saw an entire set of brass instruments on stage. There was a trombone player—that didn't fit my profile of a churchy instrument. Behind and above the stage, large organ pipes loomed over the area. I had to move farther down the pew so I could see the stage clearly, since television cameras blocked my line of vision. In fact, no matter where I moved, a camera was still blocking my view of some portion of the stage. Perhaps the positioning of the cameras is one way to encourage people to sit closer to the front.

Singers took the stage and began their songs with the help of the band. It was apparent that the younger, more attractive singers stood front and center. This was a technique more appropriate for an advertising campaign than a place of worship, I felt. And it wasn't the first time I had seen this tendency in the larger churches I'd visited. Certainly the other singers had talent as well, but they weren't positioned in front. Are good-looking people *really* much better singers?

As the time for the sermon approached, I looked to see how many people were here. For a church whose membership numbers are reported at more than forty thousand, there were plenty of vacant seats available at this service.[1] My entire row was empty, as was the one behind me and the one to my right. I suppose the rest of the church's membership comes on Sunday, but it was surprising to see such a large building with so many empty seats. The smaller churches I have visited may not have had the members or money for a larger building, but the seats were generally filled.

When the sermon finally began, Pastor Ben talked about the importance of eating a good breakfast, something seemingly unrelated to scripture. I listened intently, wondering where he was going with this. He then segued into a discussion of the Last Supper and told the story of how Peter had let Jesus down by disavowing him three times before the rooster crowed. (I finally figured out who "Pete" was on the sign outside the church.) Peter's open denial of Jesus led Pastor Ben to talk about how we, too, sometimes let God down. We don't do what we're supposed to do, but God still forgives us.

Later he brought his sermon full circle when he talked about how, after Jesus' resurrection, Jesus prepared breakfast for some of his disciples. I realized the breakfast theme from the beginning of the sermon was reappearing in a surprisingly different form. I loved that he opened with a discussion of something that seemed to be irrelevant and later managed to tie it in to his sermon. But it took far too long to get there, and it would have been nice to know where he was going with the story from the beginning.

Pastor Ben also told a personal story of how he had let God down. Years earlier, a friend of his was ridiculed for her Christianity, and instead of defending her, Ben just watched the encounter occur. Clearly, he was remorseful about what he had done (or not done), but he couldn't change the past. So he asked God for forgiveness.

As he said those words, I thought of times when I had regretted some of my own decisions. Like Pastor Ben, I would love to be able to change the past. But since I can't and since there is no way for me to be forgiven by God (since I don't believe in God), I have to learn from my mistakes and make sure it doesn't happen again. The only people I could ever ask forgiveness from are the people I have wronged. I listened carefully, but I didn't hear Pastor Ben say he had asked his friend to forgive him; he asked it only from God. I would be disappointed if that were actually the case.

I enjoyed Ben's speaking style. It would be hard to lose interest, since he was either telling a gripping story, allowing his emotions to show, or making an important point that caught my attention. If there is anything negative to be said about the way he spoke, it was that any jokes he made were not pertinent to the theme of his sermon. Ideally, the best pastors (and speakers in general) make jokes that are vital to the message—so vital, in fact, that without the jokes the sermon would lose a lot of its impact.

## HARVEST BIBLE CHAPEL, ROLLING MEADOWS, ILLINOIS

One of the largest churches I attended in the Chicago area is Harvest Bible Chapel in Rolling Meadows, Illinois. Long before I visited the church, I started wondering what I'd find there, based on what I had read on the church's Web site: "After meeting at Rolling Meadows High School for seven years, God supernaturally provided our current main church home…in Rolling Meadows in 1995."[2] If you are a churchgoing person, there might be nothing in that statement that seems odd. But for me, the word *supernaturally* was intriguing. Unless the building suddenly appeared out of nowhere, I figured there had to be a better word to describe how the congregation came to occupy its current building. In fact, the church acquired the building by purchasing it.

I drove into the parking lot of the main campus—there are two satellite campuses in surrounding suburbs—and was directed into a parking space. (Call me crazy, but the presence of parking-lot attendants has become *the* indication I'm going to enjoy a service.) The building itself looked like a convention center, enormous on the inside, with a huge auditorium and a large number of separate smaller rooms. I had planned to sit in the back of the auditorium so I could have some privacy as I took notes, but just as in the parking lot, I was ushered to a predetermined spot. This time, I was directed to a seat in the second row.

After the opening hymns, a man (not the main pastor) asked the congregation to read Psalm 25 with him. Verse 3 said, "Indeed, none who wait for you [God] shall be put to shame; they shall be ashamed who are wantonly treacherous" (ESV).

As I heard those words, it sounded like all people who were not waiting for God were said to be evil. Was that a reference to people like me? To add to my anxiety, a few minutes later when the offering was announced, the audience actually cheered in response. It worried me that I wasn't planning to give an offering. (When I visit churches, I don't make a donation.) Would my not putting anything in the offering plate attract unwanted attention? Would I be thought of as wantonly treacherous?

Once the senior pastor, James MacDonald, appeared, I was put a little more at ease. He quickly stepped down from the stage and started talking about forgiveness as he walked among those in the audience. He interacted with people sitting in the front rows, joking with them as he made his points. At other large churches I had visited, the pastors stayed on the stage, usually behind a podium. One of the main problems I had with the larger churches was the lack of intimacy between pastor and…what's the word…*pastees*? Here, though, that problem was eliminated by the pastor approaching us, *being* one of us, talking to individuals as he spoke to everyone.

While I thought this was a powerful approach to speaking, I'm not sure it was as significant for others as I imagined. Several times, when the pastor was right next to certain audience members, *they weren't watching him.* Instead, they were staring at one of the two large screens displaying a video image of the pastor. With a speaker standing right next to you, isn't it odd that you wouldn't look at him? It couldn't have been a huge inconvenience for people to turn their heads slightly to see the actual Pastor James, who was standing right there! (In fairness, there were others who looked at the pastor as he walked past them. And for them, there must have been a feeling of connection.)

What added to Pastor James's effectiveness was the emotion he made everyone feel. When he told us we needed to forgive, it wasn't enough just to agree with that idea or to say the right words. We had to first *feel* the bitterness that sometimes creeps inside our minds. I tried doing this, thinking back to a time when I did feel resentment against a person. It wasn't hard to remember the anger I had felt at the time. I also knew I didn't have those feelings anymore since I had moved on from the situation. But maybe that wasn't the case for everyone else. As I looked at faces around me, I could sense feelings of bitterness or resentment arising. It was visible in their expressions. Later on, when Pastor James finished his sermon, I noticed very few people whose eyes were not welled up with tears, as they had just gone through the process of forgiving someone.

As Pastor James gave the list of steps we needed to take to forgive someone, the first step caught me off guard. We had to name the person we wanted to forgive, and we had to be specific. This seemed odd to me. If I wanted to forgive someone, I would already be thinking of that person, and presumably God would know the person as well. However, I *did* see the value for the person who was thinking of someone he or she wanted to forgive. Saying the other person's name could help the offended party overcome an initial obstacle. So maybe this first step did have a benefit, even if it wasn't designed to alert God to the identity of the person being forgiven.

While most of the sermon was positive, I was turned off by a few of the elements. For one, an outline of the sermon was provided in the printed program. It was there for convenience, I figured, but it wasn't helpful. In fact, it seemed childish. Incomplete sentences were provided so I could fill in the blanks. Here's an example: "_____ is a fruit of forgiveness." Answer: kindness. The answers we were expected to write down were common sense. Were these really the main points we were to take away?

Beyond the obviousness, I found I didn't want to be told what to write down. I can figure out what's important for me to take away from the sermon without outside help, thank you very much. Other churches I had visited didn't do this, I felt, because the pastors were able to communicate the most important points using speaking techniques, such as vocal inflection. You knew exactly what they considered to be the key parts of the message. At Harvest Bible Chapel, each point we were to write down was preceded by the words, "Jot this down." Pastor James didn't have the voice command I had observed in the speakers at other large churches.

In addition, I found that the message itself was too often interspersed with Bible verses. (Before you fire off an e-mail, let me say I understand this was a church service, and the purpose was to teach the audience about the Bible.) My point is that the other large churches I had visited stuck to the theme of the message and kept the Bible recitations to a minimum. The pastors would say the Bible wants us to forgive, for instance, and then launch into a speech on forgiveness without going back to quote the Book. The verses were available, though, or the chapters briefly mentioned, for those who wanted to read them in greater depth. At Harvest Bible Chapel, however, it was as if the pastor felt we wouldn't believe forgiveness was mentioned in the Bible unless we heard it repeated, verbatim, from the Bible. So we were told that in *this* verse and *this* verse and *this* verse, God tells us we must act in such a way. It happened so often, in fact, that the sermon became hard to follow. I would have easily gotten the point if the church had used its video screens to list some of the pertinent verses. I didn't need to have the verses read to me.

I have heard some Christians say they prefer to attend a church whose pastor makes heavy use of verses from the Bible in his or her sermons. To them, preachers such as Joel Osteen may appear "watered down" due to the fact that he doesn't mention Bible verses as frequently as other pastors. My response would be that Osteen's messages come across more clearly to a wider audience *because* he limits the quotes from the Bible. His listeners know he is using the Bible as his reference, so he doesn't need to remind them every few sentences.

At Harvest Bible Chapel, what bothered me most was an example of forgiveness Pastor James used. He told a story about Leonardo da Vinci and prefaced the example by saying it was a true story. He talked about how Leonardo had a fight with a friend and then used the friend's face as the model for a painting of Judas. Later when he tried to paint Christ, Leonardo couldn't do it. It wasn't until he forgave his friend and redrew Judas's face that he was able to draw his famous portrait of Christ.

I later got on the Internet and searched for a reference to that story, but I came up empty. I did find a somewhat similar story that said Leonardo had once used a man's face as his model for Jesus in the painting *The Last Supper*, and years later, he used a criminal's face as the model for Judas. Surprisingly, the criminal was the same man he had used as his original model for Jesus.[3] However, according to the urban-legend-debunking Web site www.snopes .com, that story is fiction.[4] And yet the story told in church that was similar to this one was proclaimed to be factual and without any citation given. I would expect a pastor to do more thorough research, especially if he states that a story is factual. His claim that the story was true without giving a reference caused this pastor to lose credibility in my eyes.

Before the service ended, Pastor James asked those who were compelled to do so to come to the front of the auditorium, kneel on the floor, and forgive the people they had resented for so long. Quickly, a young boy—he couldn't have been more than ten years old—ran up to the front and kneeled. Several other people followed. From where I was sitting at one side of the stage, I saw more than thirty people, steeped in thought and prayer, forgiving the people in their lives. I didn't doubt their sincerity. I did wonder, however, if they would later be making phone calls or visiting those they had forgiven. Was this a temporary release from a negative part of their lives, or was it an action that would really change them for the better?

## NEW LIFE CHURCH, COLORADO SPRINGS, COLORADO

There's a sign on an empty piece of land just north of New Life Church in Colorado Springs that indicates the vacant real estate will be used for the church's expansion. It's hard to believe this church would need to grow any larger, as it's already a fourteen-thousand-person megachurch.[5] I arrived for the 11:00 a.m. service, and instead of searching for an open parking spot near the building as I would at a mall on a weekend, I ended up in the far reaches of a gigantic parking lot.

When I visited New Life, Ted Haggard was the church's senior pastor. He was also president of the National Association of Evangelicals (NAE), which purports to represent thirty million evangelical Christians in the United States.[6] A few months later, after allegations of drug use and sexual immorality surfaced, he resigned as head of the NAE and was dismissed as senior pastor at New Life.[7] Because the influence of New Life Church extends far beyond the city of Colorado Springs, I've chosen to include this report of my visit. It reflects Pastor Ted's then-current standing with the church and the NAE.

Prior to my visit, my experience in seeing Pastor Ted had been limited to two sources: One was a brief article in *Time* magazine that called him one of America's most influential evangelicals. The other was a clip from a Richard Dawkins documentary called *The Root of All Evil?* In the clip, Dawkins, a leading atheist, visits New Life Church and speaks to Ted Haggard afterward. Their discussion turns into an argument about evolution. When I watched that video clip, I sensed an air of smugness in the way Pastor Ted came across. At one point he tells Dawkins, the famous evolutionary biologist, "If you only read the books I know, and if you only knew the scientists I knew, then you would be great like me."[8]

Ted Haggard's supporters might argue that in the documentary he was simply joking with Dawkins, or perhaps his comment was taken out of context. But as far as I can tell, after repeated viewings, the tone of his voice is dead serious and the relevant part of the conversation is in context. Now, as I entered New Life Church on a Sunday morning, I would have a chance to compare Pastor Ted in person with the image I had of him based on a video interview. Was the segment in Dawkins's documentary simply edited in a way that put Pastor Ted in a bad light? I was eager to gain a first-person impression.

I waited in the church lobby as the previous service came to an end. Through the open doors, I could see the stage sitting in the middle of a huge auditorium, surrounded by rows of seats arranged almost in a full circle. This was church in the round.

As soon as the earlier service ended, people who had been standing in the lobby made a mad dash to get a good seat. I sat near the stage, in the middle of the seating arrangement. Pastor Ted was standing near the stage, laughing and talking to the members of the band and other churchgoers who had attended the earlier service. (A smile never left his face.) At the other large churches I'd visited, the pastors weren't down front mingling with the crowd after a service ended. I felt like even *I* could just walk up and talk to him… but not yet.

The band that played as people entered the auditorium was incredible. Apparently, the Desperation Band, as they're called, is an actual band based at New Life Church that tours at churches and conferences across the country. As they played, a Christian mosh pit formed in the front rows, with people jumping up and down—instead of against one another—during the choruses. I tried to get a better look at the band members, but for several minutes at a time it was hard to see past the man in front of me, whose arm was raised in praise and blocking my line of vision.

Since I couldn't see much of what was going on in front of me, I started looking around. It was amazing to see certain Christian dance moves being repeated by people at various locations in the auditorium. There was the praising with one arm reaching high, the praising with both arms raised, those same moves with separated fingers, the same moves with clenched fists, the same moves with the index fingers pointing to the heavens, the index fingers pointed while the hands moved back and forth, the same moves with elbows kept at the person's sides. Some people's eyes were open while others' were closed, and sometimes one hand would be placed on the heart. The multiple variations are too numerous to list here. I wondered if there was an unofficial competition going on between people seeking to out-praise one another.

The music lasted nearly an hour, and usually such a long period of singing gets on my nerves. But this time I didn't mind. The band was talented, and the music was catchy. Finally, Pastor Ted took the stage. This weekend, he was urging everyone to join a small group if they hadn't done so already. Outside in the lobby I had picked up the directory of different groups—the focus of the groups ranged from dirt biking to scrapbooking to playing guitar. Relatively few groups were traditional Bible studies, and Pastor Ted acknowledged this. "How about Bibles?" he joked as the church staff member in charge of small groups was describing how to join a group. "Last I heard, this was a church!"

The idea behind the small groups is that at such a large church, it's hard to feel like you have a close relationship with everyone else. The small groups provide a sense of connection to the church during the week, and on Sundays everyone can meet at church to worship together. In a way, this was like being in college. At large schools, you knew those in your dorm or maybe in the campus organizations you joined. And if there were no student groups that interested you, you could start one. You created your own experience. My college years were defined by my friends and the SWORD club I began, so I could understand the need for the small groups.

After encouraging everyone to sign up for a group, Pastor Ted began to discuss the Defining Power of a Threat. Essentially, he said, our life is shaped by the bad that happens to us. He talked about how as a young child, he had grown up in a prosperous family. However, through a set of circumstances beyond their control, his family lost their financial footing. It was after they had lost everything and were living in a small house in a different town that he saw his older brothers put their own lives on hold to help the family regroup. It was also at this point that his father turned on the television and saw Billy Graham speak, an event that changed his parents' lives and Pastor Ted's life as well.

Pastor Ted mentioned a story in 1 Samuel 11, where King Saul saved a city that was about to be attacked by the Ammonite Nahash. Prior to receiving news of the threatened attack, Saul had not been acting like a king. He had been anointed by Samuel but had not risen to the occasion. Then he was told about Nahash's threat against Jabesh, and in response to the threat, Saul resolved to do whatever it took to protect his countrymen.

In the story, Nahash offered a treaty with the people of Jabesh on the condition that Nahash would gouge out the right eye of every citizen of the city. Saul, upon hearing of the threat, cut up two oxen into small pieces and sent the bloody meat out to the rest of Israel, rallying his countrymen to come to the defense of the people of Jabesh.

As Pastor Ted told the story, he gave no indication that any of this was at all unusual or worthy of further comment. If Nahash had gouged out the right eye of every citizen of Jabesh, he said, it would have rendered the victims unable to shoot arrows in defense. But he didn't acknowledge the fact that such an attack would be torture, pure and simple. In fact, he didn't seem fazed by what I considered to be the cruel butchering of oxen. He called Saul's act a sign of power. I didn't understand how anyone could rationalize the actions of any of these people, regardless of whether it was Nahash, the enemy of Israel, or Saul, the king of Israel.

Afterward, Pastor Ted mentioned that he, too, felt angry when anyone made a disparaging remark about his church. In fact, God's Spirit welled up inside of him, and he wanted to defend New Life. I realized I feel that way when people make negative comments about atheists (it happens often), but my anger doesn't stem from God. We all want to defend the people and ideas that mean so much to us. Does Pastor Ted's passion to defend the church require a religious explanation, such as the presence of God's Spirit that stirs his passion? I would think the passion comes from his own devotion to the church he founded.

Pastor Ted went on to say he wasn't interested in always going with the crowd. (I couldn't agree more.) There were times to be bullheaded, he said, using as an example times when it's necessary to protect the moral integrity of our children. I agreed with this to a point. There are times we do need to be stubborn when standing on principle. However, Pastor Ted and other evangelical pastors I hear about in the media seem to perceive just about everything to be a threat against Christianity. Evolution is a threat. Gay marriage is a threat. A swear word uttered accidentally on television is a threat. Democrats are a threat. And so on.

I don't see how any of these things pose a threat against Christianity. If someone disagrees with you about politics, or social issues, or the matter of origins, isn't that just democracy and free speech in action? How do opposing viewpoints constitute a threat? The ideas that can be defended with reasoning or evidence will stand while others fall. But if all these issues are spun as if they *are* threats, New Life Church has an army of thousands of people who are being told to be stubborn about their beliefs. Why do Christians feel so threatened?

When one side refuses to budge, there can't be a rational discussion of the issues. Instead, there is hatred of the other side. I was offended that Pastor Ted was telling everyone to be "bullheaded" in opposing the beliefs I am passionate about. What I love about atheists is that most of us are open to discussing ideas that are contrary to what we think. If our beliefs can't hold up under further inquiry, they have to go. If atheists are willing to debate their beliefs and risk being proven wrong, why aren't Christians willing to subject their own beliefs—which they hold to be absolute truth—to the same level of scrutiny? Don't they have enough confidence in "the truth" to believe it will stand against all critics?

The nearly two-hour service finally ended, and we were asked to pray while holding our hands to heaven. (No thanks.) As people walked out of the auditorium, I decided to approach Pastor Ted. After introducing myself (not as an atheist, but simply as a visitor to the church), I asked him what he thought about his portrayal in the Dawkins documentary—was it an accurate representation? He said he hadn't seen it, which was surprising to me, as it was pretty well circulated on the Internet. He added, "Richard Dawkins is an idiot." *That was blunt,* I thought. Of course, I wanted to know why Pastor Ted felt that way. He responded that Dawkins was stubborn. I presume this is because Dawkins denies the possibility that the work of God could explain the presence of life on Earth, choosing instead to side with the evolutionary explanation. Is this stubborn? In the same clip from the documentary, Dawkins tells Pastor Ted that those who believe in science are willing to change their minds when presented with new evidence. On the other hand, the Bible never changes, even when new evidence may cast doubt on certain assertions made in the Book. Dawkins uses this reasoning to describe the beauty of science. In the documentary, however, Pastor Ted took the Bible's supposed infallibility to be a sign of its power.

In our brief conversation after church, I asked Pastor Ted if he ever entertains questions from people that challenge Christian beliefs. He said there is a Sunday-evening forum at New Life Church where people can ask questions about the sermon he gave earlier that day. In fact, he said, people can ask any question that comes to mind. Unfortunately, I couldn't stay in town long enough to attend that evening's question-and-answer session. But I appreciate that he takes time to hold such a forum. I wish more churches would follow his lead. Church members would benefit from the inclusion of such a forum, and it would certainly bring more skeptics like me to the church.

## THE MOODY CHURCH, CHICAGO, ILLINOIS

I went to The Moody Church on a Sunday evening. I had been there once before for a prayer meeting and had been astonished at the items on the prayer-request list. It seemed that everyone wanted help in areas of their lives they could fix themselves, or else the requests (at least in my mind) were irrelevant.

For example, we had been asked to pray for:

"Wisdom for Tom."

"Anonymous who is ill and cannot sleep due to neighbor playing loud music; wants a home of her own and a Christian mate."

"Anonymous believer with an unspoken request."

I had no idea how anyone could fulfill the last request, given its lack of specificity. As the people at the prayer meeting mentioned their needs, the pastor and other church members would put their hands on the requestors' shoulders, bow their heads, and pray. I felt unbelievably awkward being there; it was like I was watching a secret ceremony and I didn't know the special handshake.

I was glad that on my second visit to The Moody Church, I would be attending a regular Sunday-evening service. I was directed to the basement of the building, where I was surprised to see tables set up instead of rows of chairs. In this case, circular tables with chairs surrounding them filled the room, like a banquet hall. I was fifteen minutes early so the room was fairly empty, and the few people who were there were each sitting at a table of their own, quietly reading magazines and church literature. I found an empty table and sat down.

A man was playing piano in the front as I walked in, and another man was standing near him, moving his hands in an outward circular motion, as if he were creating a vertical snow angel. It seemed as if he had found his own method of praying. I watched him go through his movements, trying to understand the symbolism in them, but I couldn't figure it out.

Even though it was early and most of the chairs were still empty, I noticed four different races present, myself not included. The people were white, African American, East Asian, and South Asian; and as more people arrived, the various groups warmly greeted one another. I wasn't used to attending a church where the ethnic makeup was so diverse.

As the basement quickly filled up, I also noticed that nearly half the people in attendance looked as if they were *under the age of thirty*. What was this church doing that brought in so many young people? I was eager to find out.

The "snow angel man" walked over to speak to a person sitting behind me. I overheard the conversation and heard him say in an accent I couldn't place, "I don't give glory to Buddha or Krishna... I give it to God! No one else deserves it!" I heard rage in his voice when he mentioned the other deities. His comment was met with head nods up and down, signaling that the other person agreed. I understood that both men were believers in Christ, but the tone in which the first one dismissed the other religious figures worried me. I hoped the comment wasn't indicative of what I would hear for the next hour.

We began the service by singing hymns and praying. Some of the hymns were written in the program, but others were recited from memory. Later, as the others bowed their heads to pray, I looked around the room. I saw many of the people praying silently while others said their prayers out loud.

The pastor who was speaking that night, Reverend Charles M. Butler, provided a lot of historical, biblical context in order to lead up to a specific verse in John 4. We were given handouts and then told to discuss the handout with the other people at our table. Our assignment was to look at a line from John 4:24 where Jesus spoke about how people "must worship [God] in spirit and in truth." The handout asked us what the difference was between worshiping "in spirit" versus "in *the* spirit."

A man at my table, clearly a regular, led the discussion. He asked me what I thought worshiping "in spirit" meant. After a long pause, I told him it meant praying with God in mind and being focused. He smiled and nodded his head in approval. *Phew, I got it right!* I thought. The discussion continued around the table. One woman excluded herself from saying much because she said she was "just a baby Christian." By that logic, I was probably something less than an embryo.

After twenty minutes, the pastor returned to his post, where he asked various groups what they had discussed. After receiving several answers, he revealed that Jesus purposely used those words to broaden the appeal of Christianity to everyone. I didn't know how he knew Jesus' thoughts, and others seemed to wonder the same thing. They asked how Pastor Charles knew what Jesus was trying to say. His explanation made it sound as if it was something we need not concern ourselves with and we just needed to take the pastor's word for it. I felt like we were reading too much into a sentence and not looking at the meaning as a whole. Still, I accepted his analysis for the time being. Later, as the people at some of the tables continued to discuss the distinctions between the phrases, the pastor went so far as to say that because we couldn't get a handle on Jesus, it was "proof we didn't invent him!"

"Amen," the audience replied.

That was proof? The implication was that we wouldn't have purposely created a story we couldn't fully comprehend. But that explanation straddles both sides of the debate. How could Pastor Charles know what Jesus was thinking in John 4:24, and then use the difficulty of interpreting all of Jesus' statements as proof of his divinity? I would have appreciated it if the pastor had acknowledged that he was presenting his own interpretation of what he had read in John 4.

The pastor concluded the sermon by mentioning that "before we're born again, we're spiritually dead." Again, this offended me. It was as if he was saying that if we didn't accept Christ, it was because we hadn't put any serious thought into the question of our existence and purpose, or if we had done so, then we had failed to come up with the right answer. In that regard, I had never felt spiritually dead. It seemed he was distancing himself and other believers from anyone who thought differently, and I didn't see why that had to be the case. But others in the room voiced their agreement and seemed to feel better because of it. It may have been part of the reason people were attracted to The Moody Church. Here, you were a believer and you were better off than the people who chose not to believe. I wondered if this us-versus-them mentality represented the thinking of everyone in the basement that evening.

The snow-angel man came back to say good-bye to his friend sitting at the table near me. He asked the man if he believed people could speak in tongues. His friend hesitated before saying yes.

"Do you speak in tongues?"

The man laughed. "No."

I couldn't tell if the man was laughing because the idea of speaking in tongues seemed strange to him, or if he was laughing at the unexpected question itself. But I found reason for optimism in his initial hesitancy. It was as if he wanted to think about the answer before he gave it. He sounded like he wasn't entirely sure of the answer. And I hadn't heard anyone else indicate anything less than complete certainty all night.

My visits to large churches will continue in the next chapter, with three megachurches that made an especially positive impression on me—for a variety of reasons.

# Churches That Deserve Special Mention

*Positive Experiences at Three Megachurches*

I visited so many large churches that I couldn't fit the critiques into one chapter, so I've packed them into two chapters. Plus, in chapter 10—where I discuss what it would take to convert me—I include a critique of the only church that invited me back to take part in a weekend's worth of sermons.

In this chapter, I'll highlight three megachurches that made a big impression on me. Even if you've never attended these churches, you may already know quite a bit about them. Their impact goes well beyond the walls of the individual churches and the cities where they are located.

## MARS HILL BIBLE CHURCH, GRANDVILLE, MICHIGAN

On my way to the Grand Rapids area to visit Mars Hill Bible Church, I drove past road signs telling me I was entering "Gd Rapids." "Gd" might as well have been shorthand for God, considering the many churches that are located in this area. But Mars Hill Bible stands out, and not for the usual reasons. It stands out by being next to impossible to find. Located behind a bowling alley and a Pizza Hut, next to a YMCA, and inside what used to be a shopping mall, a door that had the church's name on it finally came into view. There were no flashy signs greeting me as I drove into the parking lot, and no long entry roads carrying me across hundreds of acres of church campus. You pretty much have to know already that the church is there or you'll miss it.

On the Sunday I visited, there were plenty of people who *did* know the church was there. Long lines of cars waited to find parking spots. I had read that ten thousand people attend Mars Hill Bible Church on any given weekend. I think most of them showed up for the same service I did.

Mars Hill is the only "emerging" church I visited during the research I conducted for this book. Emerging churches are typically led by younger leaders and appeal primarily to young adults. They often adopt worship styles, preaching styles, and philosophies of ministry that contrast dramatically with more traditional churches. But even though Mars Hill is an emerging church, it's also a megachurch.

Well, maybe not—there's no bookstore or café inside. And no escalators.

Once you enter this converted shopping mall (no pun intended), you find that the former stores are now used for childcare areas and welcome centers. The incredibly large auditorium that serves as the church's gathering place has a small stage in the middle, with seats surrounding it in rows that reach to the back of the room. A four-sided box hangs right above the stage, and each side presents a large video screen visible to one-quarter of the room.

This is the church headed by Rob Bell, the author of *Velvet Elvis* and *Sex God,* and a man who had just returned from a nationwide speaking tour on the topic Everything Is Spiritual. His wildly popular lecture tour covered the country, from Sacramento to New York City.

I found a seat near the front row. It was still a half hour before the service was to begin, and the platform held only a couple of acoustic guitars, a piano, some microphones, and a couple of crawling babies. No one seemed to mind. Their mothers sat on the edge of the stage, talking. There were many babies in the auditorium, in fact. Not only that, but there were as many teenagers there as you'd expect to find at an actual shopping mall. This church appears to be run entirely by people under the age of forty.

When I spotted Rob Bell, my first thought was that he looks like he belongs in the band Weezer. Either that, or he should be giving poetry readings. That Sunday he had bleached-blond hair and was wearing dark-rimmed glasses, khakis, and a white shirt underneath a sweater vest. Meanwhile, high-school and college-age students were filling the seats around me, and I overheard some strange conversations.

"My Bible feels naked because I just got a new one," the girl behind me told her friend. I assume she meant she had not had time to underline her favorite verses or write notes in the margins. She added later that she might come back to the evening service with another person, but "five hours of church might be overkill."

*You have no idea,* I wanted to tell her.

As Rob Bell ran up on stage, he was greeted with applause and cheers. He had been gone for several weeks on his speaking tour, and this was his first Sunday back "home." The parishioners were glad to see him again.

Rob introduced two guests—friends of his—who are musicians who work with an African gospel choir. Rob wanted them to help Mars Hill Bible Church learn new ways of worship. The two men grabbed their guitars, walked up to the microphones (I was facing their backs), and introduced the song they were about to sing. As they talked, the video monitor above them displayed the lyrics in a foreign language. The guitarist walked the audience through the pronunciations, and before he began singing, he joked, "Let us speak in tongues for a bit."

Once the songs finished, the lead pastor, Don Golden, joined Rob on stage and made a few introductory comments. Pastor Don asked the audience if anyone subscribed to the *Grand Rapids Press* newspaper. After an unenthusi-astic response, Pastor Don responded, "Yeah, me neither." He went on to say, though, that a headline in that day's edition grabbed his attention. The head-line said that the population of those living in poverty in Grand Rapids num-bers one in five. If this is a church that cares about the poor, he said, the people needed to read this newspaper article. However, he didn't say anything at that time about what actions the church would take to help remedy the situ-ation, which was disappointing.

Finally, Rob began to speak, giving the crowd an update on his tour. He said it went well, though from his remarks I gathered it was a grueling sched-ule. He talked about the different cities he visited—Chicago, New York, Las Vegas ("Dear God, help us all," he remarked), among others. The people in the audience know their pastor is on the rise. He's not a full-blown celebrity. Not yet. He still belongs to them, and they were thankful to have him back at Mars Hill. Rob thanked them for their support throughout the speaking tour and ended his story by mentioning that the tour bus brought his family back to Michigan before taking off for its next destination: Los Angeles, to pick up singer Justin Timberlake. ("R.B. and J.T.—Best Friends Forever," he joked.)

He then told us to go directly to John 20 and read along with him. The video monitors showed us the verse and page number we should be going to if we had borrowed one of the church's NIV Bibles, which was helpful. What followed was an interpretation of the time near Christ's resurrection that might be the funniest analysis I'll ever hear from a pastor. Rob Bell didn't make jokes about the serious situation that is occurring in this story. Rather, it was the way he interpreted what is going on in the story. In this case, he made the point that the writer, John, constantly referred to himself without explicitly doing so, calling himself "the other disciple." The audience began to laugh every time they saw it happening. (Here's an example: "So Peter and the *other disciple* started for the tomb. Both were running, but the *other disciple* outran Peter.... Finally, *the other disciple, who had reached the tomb first,* also went inside."[1]) Rob read through the whole passage, line by line, but when he wanted to add a footnote, he stopped and spoke to the audience.

He reminded us that as we read we must constantly ask: can we see ourselves in these stories?

The theme of the sermon was to focus on living your own life and doing what God has planned for you, instead of trying to live someone else's life. Just as God had given John and Simon Peter each his own purpose to fulfill.

Rob asked us to turn to 1 Samuel 8, then 1 Kings 9, then Exodus 20, then another passage and another. The point was to show that the theme of people having a God-given purpose recurs in the Bible in various sections. Samuel, Solomon, and Moses all had specific tasks to carry out. Rob's approach reminded me of literary analysis I did in high school with works of fiction—comparing one text to another to identify common themes and recurring patterns of thought. The page turns went by extremely quickly, and sometimes it was hard to keep up. But by the time Rob was done, his point had been made. The theme shows up throughout the Bible.

Earlier I mentioned that Pastor James at Harvest Bible Chapel did something similar, zipping through a large number of Bible verses. However, Rob's "look at how interesting this is" tone resonated with me much more than Pastor James's "it's in the Bible; trust me" tone. At Mars Hill we took time to read these verses together and understand how the theme applied.

However, it would have been helpful if he had also mixed in some references to current-day people who were trying to be someone they are not. It also would've helped to point out that what was happening in the biblical stories still occurs in the present day—and perhaps why it's often difficult for people to live the lives they believe God has planned for them.

Rob Bell is a speaker like no other I've ever seen. His quirks make him a compelling person to watch. It's the way he talks to everyone as if he were face to face with you in a coffee shop, not as if he's delivering a lecture. It's the way he strongly pronounces the first S in Je-Sus. It's how he can find humor in situations that wouldn't otherwise warrant laughter. I observed some of these things as he gave his sermon, and also as I talked to him later. I could also anticipate some of it from reading parts of his book *Velvet Elvis*.

When the service ended, I waited in line to leave the auditorium. In the meantime, I realized there had not been a communion service or an offering plate passed around. Instead of a collection, we were reminded that if we'd like to contribute money, there were "joy boxes" in the back.

Rob and I had a chance to talk before his evening sermon that same day. I wanted to call him Pastor Rob, but even after watching him preach, I couldn't bring myself to use such a formal title. It doesn't fit his image. Our discussion delved into a variety of topics, and I could write at length about the interesting comments he made, but instead I'll focus on just two remarks.

When I asked about the unique nature of the building, a former shopping mall without signs to announce its presence, Rob said he wanted the church to be full of the die-hards, the believers who really wanted to be there. There was no need to advertise the church or post signs. If people wanted to find Mars Hill Bible Church, they could locate the information they needed to guide them there. Churches shouldn't be gaining members based on good marketing, he felt. Not only that, the building was just that—a physical space. Forget the fact that this was an old mall with little décor. The real church expands well past the building into the community, and that's what Rob wanted to see happen.

I also asked him what the response had been from other churches in the area to his brand of worship. Rob responded that the reactions went across the spectrum. He said some people were "organizing rallies to denounce me and writing pamphlets against me." Why did that happen? Maybe because Rob was pushing aside common traditions, practices, and symbols of faith for what he saw to be truer Christianity. In any case, he said he had two options: "I can throw stones back, or I can use it to become a certain kind of forgiving, loving person…and I don't claim to have that mastered, but it is a challenge." It was an ideology I appreciated. It was also one I had learned several times in my life, first in Jainism, and later in atheism. And while Rob and I may disagree on the divinity of Jesus, I didn't sense any air of superiority from him. We were new friends talking about serious issues. To Rob, that was the essence of what a Christian should be.

## LAKEWOOD CHURCH, HOUSTON, TEXAS

It's 10:45 on a Sunday morning in Houston, and I'm sitting on what I'm pretty sure was once the three-point arc for the Houston Rockets. Now it's the carpeted floor of the huge worship area for Lakewood Church, and the arena is as crowded as it would be for an NBA game. The upper-deck seats are virtually empty right now as people first fill in the floor-level and lower-level seating to be as close to the stage as possible. However, by the time the service is well underway, most of the balcony-level seats are filled as well.

A slowly spinning globe occupies the back of the stage with waterfalls on either side. It's a beautiful backdrop. The choir is positioned on both sides of the stage, preparing to sing. In the back of the arena hangs a huge American flag, and Joel Osteen is preparing to take the stage. I've been looking forward to this church visit for a long time.

I may be an atheist, but I love Joel. My mom is a Jain, and she loves Joel. She doesn't read many books, but she borrowed his best-selling book, *Your Best Life Now,* from a colleague at work. My mom and I discovered Joel Osteen separately. She told me about this amazing speaker she had seen on television, and I realized she was referring to the same guy I had seen while channel surfing one night. I stopped switching channels when I came across him.

I knew he was a Christian pastor, but something about the way he spoke appealed to me. I loved that he could talk about Christian *values* without necessarily relying on the Bible to do so. He told his audience to spend more time with their families, to be loyal, and to be grateful for today, among his many topics. At some point in his sermon, he would quote scripture or tell a story directly from the Bible, but for the most part he got his message across without emphasizing a lot of Bible verses. While I disagreed with the emphasis I often heard him place on waiting for God to provide (I'd prefer taking action instead), the values Joel espouses are the same ones I try to follow—we both want to live a happier and fuller life, we both want to have healthy, lasting marriages (I look forward to someday getting married), we both know personal responsibility is vital to achieving a healthy, fulfilling life (though Joel believes God will help us achieve that goal).

The things I enjoy about Joel's sermons are the same motivational-speaker qualities that lead some Christians to refer to his sermons as Christianity-lite and argue that he isn't preaching Christian doctrine as strongly as he should. Still, he has an undeniable mass appeal, and it led to Lakewood's becoming the largest church in the country—with a weekly attendance of more than thirty thousand people.[2]

As the choir began the praise songs, the audience stood to sing along. I might have been thinking this atmosphere was more like a rock concert than a Sunday-morning service, but the metaphor soon became literal. The crowd sang and clapped as if they were listening to their favorite band. Unlike the typical guitars-and-drums setup I'd seen at other large churches, Lakewood has a small-but-complete orchestral ensemble. It was also easy to notice that everyone here seemed much more dressed up than I'd observed at other mega-churches. There weren't many jeans-wearing parishioners in the crowd, much less men wearing shorts. In fact, many of the guys were wearing ties! The women were in long dresses and many wore makeup. Why was that? Perhaps it was the fact that this sermon will be broadcast across the nation, or maybe it was just peer pressure, knowing that everyone else will be dressed for church, so to speak.

The lead singer on stage was one of the most energetic worship leaders I have seen—and she had a great voice. She made sure the audience was involved. In fact, some in the congregation got a little *too* involved. Every time the singer took a breath, a woman behind me took the opportunity to scream out phrases containing the words *Jesus, adore,* and *deliver.* They had nothing to do with the song lyrics, so I assume she was talking to herself, or to God. But at the same time, her outbursts were distracting. And loud.

Nearly an hour after the first song began, Joel took the stage to begin his sermon. He told a joke, then told us to open our Bibles (just about everyone but me had brought his or her own copy) to 1 John 1:9. The passage discussed how, if we confess our sins, we will be forgiven. However, outside of an allusion to a biblical story later on, it was the last time I heard Joel mention a specific chapter and verse. And even the verse from 1 John was referred to only briefly, as one of the many ways we can get ourselves out of a rut. What followed, instead, was a series of stories and lessons we needed to remember.

One of Joel's most appealing qualities is that he tells stories about himself and his wife, Victoria. Sometimes the stories are revealing and even embarrassing; sometimes they are self-deprecating. But they are always honest. I can't recall hearing any other pastor talk so much about his or her private life. As Joel spoke in front of an arena full of people, I felt like I *knew* him, at least a little bit. Consequently, I was more interested in what he had to say.

One of his points that morning was that we have to listen to God when He speaks to us. In other words, whenever we hear a voice telling us, *This is wrong,* or, *I need to do this,* we need to listen. If we were spending more money than we had, we needed to stop. If our friends were dragging us down, we needed to let them go. If we had a friendship or marriage that wasn't going well, we needed to fix the problem. Each time he brought up a point, he motioned to his stomach, indicating we should follow our gut.

Every time he did this, I kept thinking that since God doesn't exist for me, there has to be some other explanation for why people have these inner promptings. I have them too. When I was a student teacher in a math classroom, I had an experience when a student asked me a simple question from the previous night's homework. What should have been a quick explanation of the correct answer turned into a disastrous several minutes where I drew an incorrect diagram on the board and proceeded to confuse several students in the process. When I talked to my cooperating teacher after the class, I could have lied and told him I had a hard time understanding the student or that I misunderstood the question. A lie would have made the situation much less uncomfortable. But inside, I knew I should just be truthful and deal with the awkwardness that would follow. So I did. I told the teacher I hadn't looked at the homework assignment and was thrown off by the student's question. We talked about it, and the outcome wasn't too bad. I learned a lesson from the whole situation.

If I'm an atheist and I get these inner promptings to be ethical, then what's so special about hearing that inner voice? If I need to make a tough decision, I tend to go with my first instinct. Whenever I consider telling a lie, there is a voice telling me not to. But is that God? I don't think so. Don't we already know it's a good thing to repair a broken relationship, or to avoid situations that could result in our harm, or to be honest and not steal, and to not hurt others?

Meanwhile, the audience at Lakewood Church seemed to hang on each of Joel's words. As he spoke, he became more and more passionate. At one point, the emotions must have been too much for him; he had to cover his face and look away from the audience and cameras. It was evident he was weeping over how powerful he felt God was, and he didn't want to lose his composure in front of the audience.

You might expect that an atheist would assume that Joel's losing it and sobbing in front of thousands of people was an insincere gesture, a speaker's ploy to hold his audience. With another pastor, I might see myself thinking that. But here I felt none of that. It was evident the audience was moved along with him. During the pause, many people cried out, "We love you, Joel," and clapped so he could take a second to regain his poise.

He joked about how he had been so close to finishing the sermon without losing it but couldn't do it. I appreciated his humility. It's difficult for any speaker to get back on track after being rattled, but Joel finished his sermon without any other interruptions.

Thinking about it now, several days after I visited Lakewood Church, I still feel that his tears were genuine. I can't be cynical about it, because I have watched him preach many times before on television and also via his video podcasts. He doesn't need to resort to false emotions to move an audience. He has the power to do that with his words alone.

Before he finished, Joel asked us to rise if we were visitors to Lakewood so the audience could clap for us. I remained seated but saw quite a large number of visitors standing. This wasn't just a church; it was a tourist attraction!

Afterward, visitors to Lakewood were encouraged to meet Joel and Victoria outside in the lobby, and I got there as fast as I could. I was far back in the line, but I held on to a copy of his book *Your Best Life Now.* I knew we wouldn't have much time to talk, so when he finally came to me, I let it all out:

"Joel, I'm an atheist, and my mom, well, she's not Christian, but we're huge fans!"

The look on his face said, *Then what are you doing here...?* But he graciously autographed the book for my mom, shook my hand, and moved on to others waiting in the long line.

I can't imagine what it's like to be both a pastor and a celebrity, where weekend services are attended by church members, local newcomers, visiting tourists, and a wide television audience. But Joel and his wife took the time to meet as many people as possible after each one of their weekend services, and I appreciated that.

Even if Joel's preaching may not be as Bible-focused as some Christians would prefer, he wears his Christianity on his sleeve and encourages everyone else to do likewise. I would say to his detractors that so many of the people I sat near or passed in the lobby had brought their own Bibles instead of borrowing a church-issued one to use during the service. So much for saying the Bible doesn't matter here.

Even though I don't believe in the God that Joel does, I still walked out of Lakewood Church with the knowledge that thousands of people were going to have a better day, and maybe even a better life, after hearing him speak. That might be the key to making Sunday-morning services—and the church in general—more appealing, even to outsiders. All people are looking for a better life, whether they believe in God or not.

## WILLOW CREEK COMMUNITY CHURCH, SOUTH BARRINGTON, ILLINOIS

On a Saturday evening, I drove from my apartment in Chicago to the northwest suburb of South Barrington to visit Willow Creek Community Church. They have three weekend services, and this was the first. The *Church Report* magazine stated that Willow Creek (with Pastor Bill Hybels) ranked at the top of a list of "The 50 Most Influential Churches in America." The ranking, released in July 2006, tallied the votes of two thousand church leaders across the country. Willow Creek beat out other influential churches, including Rick Warren's, Joel Osteen's, T. D. Jakes's, and the churches of a number of other Christian leaders whose names were familiar even to me.[3]

As I turned off the main road to enter the church campus, I could envision how the church got its name: *it's a community all by itself.* A large lake and smooth road open up into a large network of buildings and a parking lot that was nearly full when I arrived. And I was early! I parked my car in one of the few open spots, picked up my tape recorder and notepad, and walked toward the main doors, suddenly realizing I was wearing nearly all black clothing. It wasn't intentional; I had just picked out some nice pants and a button-up shirt from my closet, forgetting that black may not be the clothing of choice at any church.

I feared I would stand out among the churchgoers donning their Sunday best, but as I walked toward the church, I was shocked to see the Christians wearing clothes otherwise reserved for a trip to the grocery store. While some did wear shirts and ties or nice dresses, many men wore jean shorts, and women wore tank tops. At first, I thought it was a sign of disrespect, but as I stepped inside, I could understand how people would be more comfortable wearing their normal, everyday clothes. They could come to church and still be themselves.

Once inside, I felt like people were staring at me. Again, my skin color was the first thought that came to my mind. Or maybe they knew I was an atheist. Was it because I was walking alone? Most of the people entering the church were walking with one or two other people.

I went up the escalator to the second level of seats and picked a spot toward the side. I sat in an empty row and got ready to take notes on what I was about to hear. According to the program I was given (a glossy, full-color pamphlet), today's sermon would deal with how we must wait for God to deliver us and how that is sometimes difficult.

As the guitars, drums, and singers finished playing the introductory music, the pastor who was speaking that evening, Mike Breaux, came out and gave a brief statement about how we are often impatient in our lives. He asked everyone to turn to a neighbor and tell the other person what made us impatient. A man in front of me leaned over and asked me what I thought. I told him I sometimes got annoyed when people moved slower than I did in any situation. He responded that he never liked standing in a line. It was a simple interaction, but as we talked a little more, I discovered he was another pastor at Willow Creek. He was my "in" for any questions! A journalist couldn't have hoped for a better opportunity. I asked him if he would be willing to answer some of my questions once the sermon was over, and he graciously accepted.

On the stage, Mike Breaux was wearing jeans! (I no longer felt anxious about what I was wearing.) His title—teaching pastor—had me incorrectly thinking he was a sort of apprentice. It was from my new pastor friend that I learned Willow Creek has nearly two hundred fifty pastors, an astounding number, each of whom has a specialty. Pastor Mike's "gift" was communication, so he preaches. Other pastors specialize in marriage counseling. The pastor sitting in front of me said he helps churchgoers deal with their finances.

The sermon series had begun weeks earlier, and Pastor Mike referred to lessons that were covered in previous sermons; however, I was able to catch up without a problem. I listened to him explain the principles of waiting for our prayers to be answered.

1. God does have a plan for our lives, and He has a much better view from above.
2. God is always with you, working even when you wait in the dark.
3. God's plan is to have the right person in the right place for His right purposes.

Interspersed with these lessons was the biblical story of Joseph. I hadn't seen the musical about the "amazing technicolor dreamcoat," much less heard of the story. In short, Pastor Mike explained that Joseph had a dream that his family would one day bow down to him, which elicited jealousy from his brothers. They hated him and plotted to kill him but instead chose to sell him. (That wasn't good.) He ended up in Egypt in the hands of a man named Potiphar. Potiphar's wife propositioned Joseph, but he refused her advances. Still, he was falsely accused of attempted rape and jailed as a result. (That's even worse than being sold.) Joseph was in prison for several years before finally being released; he soon earned a post that made him a ruler, second in power only to Pharaoh. Some of his brothers later came to Egypt hoping to buy grain during a famine, and since Joseph was second in command over the entire nation, this fulfilled the dream Joseph had had when he was young.[4]

The point he made was that despite the horrendous trials Joseph had to go through, the Bible explained that he continued to have faith. Joseph waited, and so should we. The message resonated since I knew I had given up my faith rather quickly after I moved from Knoxville, Tennessee, back to the Chicago area as a teenager. Had I waited before discarding my faith, might I have held on to my religion?

It was interesting to hear that Joseph had persevered wherever he was, despite the situation, due to his faith. Ironically, while I couldn't compare my life to Joseph's, I knew I had overcome my own struggles only after I *lost* my faith. When I was religious, I thought God was responsible for my family's having to move to a different state. If this was some sort of test, I wanted no part of it. I thought God wasn't on my side, and I stopped believing in Him. But once I lost my faith, I understood there were events in life that were beyond my control and I had to take responsibility for how I reacted to the situation. When my family moved, I had to make new friends and find new passions because God wasn't going to do it for me. I was responsible for solving my own problems.

As I heard the story of Joseph, my logical side kicked in. There were so many points the pastor was not raising! Pastor Mike made it clear there was no time limit for waiting for God to deliver, and that God's plan did not always match our own. He added that when the good did finally happen, it wasn't a coincidence; there was no other explanation but that God had intervened.

To me, this approach is like playing the lottery. You may never win anything. However, Pastor Mike might as well have said if you do win the lottery, it's never because of luck—God must have played a role in it. Of course, if you didn't win the lottery, it wasn't because God was against you. You just had to have faith and wait. I wanted to know why a "success" meant God was working on our side, but failure was not blamed on God. How could one be God's doing but not the other? Pastor Mike told us God was with Joseph in the prison cell and God was also there before that episode, when Joseph was sold into slavery.

I didn't feel that this was a stretch for the audience to believe since Joseph's dreams came true in the end. But I had to wonder, *If Joseph had not been taken out of prison, would we still interpret that as part of God's divine plan?* Pastor Mike's interpretation was a win-win situation for Christians, with doubters having no opportunity to show the reasoning was flawed. If God is there in the bad times and the good times both—if He is working no matter what a person's circumstances might be—then there is no room for chance or coincidence, or even the simple effects of a person's acting in a certain way to achieve a certain outcome. Aren't we responsible to live wisely, in a way that will produce good outcomes based on living ethically?

I hear stories all the time about innocent people being executed or people whose lives are ruined by natural disasters (frequently referred to as "acts of God," no less!). I didn't see how God was with these people whose lives were destroyed.

That wasn't the only part of the sermon that made me question what I heard. Pastor Mike gave us examples of people he knew or who had written to him describing how they had waited (or were currently waiting) for deliverance and how their perseverance helped them through rough times. One of the examples was a man who was in jail for committing a white-collar crime. While he was in prison, he found a new purpose. He was now teaching GED classes to other inmates, and he knew that when he got out of prison, he could live life in a more positive, Christian way. I couldn't help but wonder why the man couldn't have used his life for good from the beginning, instead of first committing a crime and having to learn the hard lesson in prison. Was jail part of God's plan for him? As far as I could see, it was simply his human weakness and greed that landed him in prison.

Unfortunately, there was no forum where I could raise such questions. I couldn't run up to the pastor afterward, nor would I have felt right asking a random stranger sitting near me. At a smaller church, I might have had this opportunity, though even at those churches I never saw anyone going up to the pastor afterward with a list of questions.

Still, as I watched people in the audience taking notes and laughing at the pastor's jokes, I kept thinking of the stereotypical image I'd had of larger evangelical churches. What happened to the gay bashing and calls for knocking down the wall between church and state? These were attitudes and views I expected to see emphasized. But I didn't hear any such sentiments expressed at Willow Creek Community Church. I wondered why secular people pointed to the church as the focal point for the opposition on social issues. I realized, *This was not a dangerous place for a secular person.* In fact, I enjoyed Pastor Mike's talk. I could take a secular message back with me: even when I was going through a rough time, it didn't mean that was the end of the story. I didn't think God would help me, but certainly, I could help myself. And if the problem went beyond my ability to solve, I could always turn to my friends and family. In any case, I could have confidence in my own abilities and work hard to get myself out of any hole. I wasn't sure if that was a message Pastor Mike would approve of, but it worked for me.

We finished the service with a few songs of praise. I'd heard a number of songs during my previous church visits, and for the most part, they all sounded similar. This time, though, they sang a song called "Blessed Be Your Name," and it was familiar to me. When they sang the line, "Every blessing you pour out," I quietly recited, "I'll turn back to praise…"[5] Oh, boy…I knew the words to a Christian song. It was a sure sign that church had become a part of my weekly ritual.

Once the sermon was over, the pastor sitting in front of me stayed behind to answer some of my questions. I asked him whether jail was really a part of God's plan for Joseph in the Bible and also for the man convicted of a white-collar crime. He responded that God was more interested in our character than our happiness, and sometimes it might take something traumatic, such as a prison sentence, to help a person see that. Sometimes, he said, people just did stupid things. God's beauty was to "mold" His plan for us around our own actions. I didn't agree with him, but I thought his explanation was better than the one Pastor Mike had presented.

I asked him why I wasn't hearing any of the conservative ideology I expected to hear at an evangelical church. The pastor responded that the church did offer classes for certain controversial topics during the week, but that Willow Creek, unlike some other megachurches, made sure that when a topic wasn't written in black and white in the Bible, the topic was addressed in a way that allowed for discussion. Murder was a black-and-white issue in the Bible. There were no discussions about whether it was right or wrong. "Are Intelligent Design and gay rights black-and-white issues?" I asked. No, he said. Willow Creek brought in experts to deal with these issues, since there were so many nuances.

Unfortunately, from what I saw on the Willow Creek Web site and in the printed program, the experts that were brought in to discuss these issues seemed to come only from the conservative side; the time for debate only occurred as part of the question-and-answer sessions following a formal presentation. That was disappointing to me. Why perpetuate the idea that believing in evolution is tantamount to being an atheist when even leading scientists who are Christian, such as Francis Collins, have said there are ways to believe in both God and a form of evolution?[6]

That said, I wasn't expecting the church to bring in *only* a proponent of evolution. But when social or scientific issues like that arose, I would like to see a church with the financial capabilities of Willow Creek bring in experts from differing sides of the issue to at least hold a formal debate. Are they afraid a proevolution scientist might make too many good points?

Still, the service I attended was a pleasant one. It's no surprise why twenty thousand people show up at Willow Creek Community Church and its satellite locations on any given weekend.[7] The last time I had attended this church, on a Wednesday night, I had come to a service for people who already believe. The weekend services, in contrast, are aimed more at newcomers and "spiritual seekers," and are not as heavy-laden with theology. After both of my visits, I left with a feeling of satisfaction. Yes, I disagreed with the church on important social issues, as well as its religious beliefs. Still, if any church were to convert me, I felt it would be a place such as Willow Creek. It wasn't a fire-and-brimstone service. It wasn't a worship-God-out-of-fear-of-hell service. It was a place where I could think about the message after I left.

If any church had a chance of making me come back for more, it was Willow Creek.

# What Works on Sunday Morning and What Doesn't

## Suggestions to Help You Reach Out to Non-Christians

During the months I was doing research for this book, I attended churches of all sizes and was exposed to a number of different denominations. I visited churches in four states, in cities and suburbs and in one small town. I experienced formal worship, informal, and in-between. After attending a large number of services, I realized there are things churches can do to help make God real to visitors—or at least, to help people better understand the idea of God and why they should reexamine their beliefs and give Him careful consideration. After all, if people can't get this sort of input in a church, where are they supposed to look for it?

The churches in America have tremendous potential to do good and to reach out to nonreligious people in ways that could have an amazing impact. In many of the churches I visited I noticed things that consistently worked very well. But too many times I saw churches repeating stereotypes and supporting ideas that seem to go against the very core of what I understood Christianity to stand for. One common attitude justified intolerance rather than emphasizing Christian love. Another contradictory emphasis was a narrow focus on meeting needs within the church, rather than an outward focus on how the church could assist everyone in the community. Within minutes of entering a new church or upon hearing the pastor's first words, I could almost predict the things I would encounter that would fail to connect.

In this chapter I'll summarize both the good and the bad, but not to complain or to hold myself up as an expert. I am simply telling you how a variety of churches came across to me—a young adult who is a well-educated atheist open to any compelling evidence for the existence of God. If your church is interested in making Christianity real to spiritual outsiders, then I am your target audience. I want to give you honest feedback that will help you do a better job of having a conversation with people like me.

Bear in mind, I notice things regular churchgoers may overlook, since they have grown accustomed to their services over the years. For instance, I know from experience that singing praise songs with repeated choruses is not only a common feature of worship services but apparently a widely enjoyed part of the service for most who attend. However, I consistently noticed a lot of people showing up late for church. And I know of at least one Christian family that *deliberately* arrives late on Sunday morning in order to avoid the lengthy and repetitive songs. In this case, something I found personally irritating apparently is also bothersome to some Christian worshipers.

My suggestions in this chapter grow out of primary research. I would guess I've spent more time in church in the last seven months than many Christians have, outside of pastors and other church staff members. It's understandable that regular attendees would be unaware of many of the problems I saw. And if I were a personal friend of the pastors of the churches I visited, I might be less inclined to offer the critiques you'll see in this chapter. The fact that I am a visitor frees me to speak candidly and prevents personal biases based on friendship from coloring my perceptions and observations.

As you read my analysis, don't assume I'm simply an angry atheist out to tear down your church—or churches similar to yours. First, I'm not angry. And second, I wouldn't be doing this if I didn't want to help Christians develop a clearer view of themselves and the way they come across to the people they say they want to reach. Remember, I'm at the center of your target audience.

Having said that, let me assure you I found much to affirm and support in what the churches are doing. I'll begin my comments with the positive qualities I want to emphasize. Only later will I touch on some negative aspects of churches that would discourage me from going back for a second visit. I have focused on the church services and how they come across to a spiritual seeker who shows up to examine and absorb what is being presented. Since I am an atheist interested in the Christian faith, that's essentially what I've been doing ever since my eBay experiment began.

No one knows better than an atheist that major questions about life's meaning, reality, the universe, the conflict of good and evil—the list goes on and on—remain unanswered. We don't pretend to have the final answers on everything. So when I go to church, I'm as open as the next person to examining and weighing the answers that are offered. In that spirit, let's look at what I found in church that consistently *worked* and, often, worked very well.

## What Churches Are Doing Right

To give you a macro view of what stood out as positive forces in most of the churches I visited, I've narrowed it down to five general areas that caught my attention. I'll begin with the most obvious, the speaker on stage.

## Topnotch Preachers and Speakers

The one element that stood out most noticeably during every church visit was the quality and effectiveness of the speakers. Some of the pastors were incredibly gifted. Most were above average. But a few bored me (and frankly, they bored many of the people around me) from start to finish. When a pastor is genuinely funny (not just telling a joke for the sake of lightening the mood), has a message that is relevant to everyday life, and knows how to get that message across in a powerful way, that church will attract people who may not otherwise be interested in Christianity.

It's not surprising to me that the megachurches recruit the best speakers as pastors and, on occasion, as guest speakers. They certainly have the money to do so. But even leaders of smaller churches would do well to take a refresher course in public speaking. I assume that most pastors have a great deal of biblical knowledge. But does having that knowledge matter if no one wants to listen? Think about the best and worst teachers you had in college. The best ones made you want to listen—they had a way of making the subject come alive. They ignited a passion inside you. The best teachers (and the best preachers) connect with something inside you that makes you not just listen but moves you to *act*. It's not an overstatement to say the greatest teachers change their students' lives. The same is true of great pastors.

Having said that, however, the weakest speakers fail to ignite either interest or a change in the way a person thinks, feels, or lives. The worst preachers I observed stood in one place, read to us what we could easily have read on our own, and lacked individuality, energy, and a memorable delivery. If I used those words to describe a college professor, no student would willingly sign up for that prof's course. Likewise, no one wants to go back to a church with that kind of speaker at the podium on Sunday morning.

Pastors who are unsure of which category they belong to would serve themselves well by videotaping during their sermons, but instead of having the cameras focus on the pastor, turn the cameras toward the audience. Are the people attentive? Are they taking notes? Are they smiling? Or are they staring at the same page in the day's program for extended periods of time?

## Community Outreach

Some of the churches I visited made it very clear how they were helping their communities and the rest of the world. One of the churches I attended during my initial visits following the eBay auction was located in a poor area on the south side of Chicago. That church provides free tutoring for every third-grade student living in that zip code—regardless of the student's religious affiliation. Windsor Village United Methodist Church, a church I visited in Houston, Texas, led the way in revitalizing an entire neighborhood in an economically depressed section of Houston. The church has brought economic development, new homes, educational opportunities, social services, health services, and a larger employment base to an area that had been in decline. Some churches assist single moms and abused women, or help those who otherwise have no access to medical care, or provide job-skills training and other practical assistance for people who need help.

On the other hand, some church bulletins announce women's quilting night. I have nothing against quilting, and I know that catering to the preferences of atheists isn't the primary focus of any church. Nor should it be. But when we atheists see how a church is making a positive difference locally and globally by meeting crucial physical needs of people, it's hard to argue that churches are not a valuable part of society or that they should not be supported in their work. In fact, I wish more atheist groups would emulate that aspect of these churches' missions.

Building a new neighborhood is not possible for smaller churches, of course. They don't always have the manpower, the expertise, or the money. However, it is still possible for members of smaller churches to volunteer at soup kitchens or host charity functions. Better yet, gather members of your church—along with members of other churches, temples, synagogues, and mosques in your area—and do some community service together in your city. You would be serving the community while getting to know people of other faiths who share a commitment to helping people.

A group of people from a church outside Chicago fixed up the house of a WWII veteran who was unable to do the work himself. The church's name wasn't associated with the project. The leader of one of the church's small groups simply called the town's mayor and asked about needs in the community that could be addressed by a group of volunteers.

When churches launch charitable and humanitarian efforts, I have noticed one problem. Many of the efforts seem to be focused on helping those who are Christians or those who seem likely to convert. For example, when churches build private schools—sometimes in an underserved part of a city— the schools are Christian in nature. Whenever I hear this, I wonder why the churches that have resources and an interest in education can't help out a public school in a part of town where students are struggling. With that approach, they could help out all children, regardless of their religious background. I would imagine that teachers generally welcome caring adults who come in to tutor, to help with art class or music class, or who help organize classroom parties to celebrate certain holidays. Why do churches tend to create something that is separate and specifically "Christian," rather than pitching in to help improve the work being done at existing schools in the neighborhood?

The same church on the south side of Chicago that provided free tutoring for third graders, which I mentioned earlier, also delivered thirty thousand Bibles to every home in that zip code. There's a clear impact that can be made through the tutoring program. However, a book teaching children how to improve their study skills would have helped the children with their education much more than a Bible could. (Remember, I'm giving you a perspective from outside the church.)

My bigger point is that the more work churches do for *everyone,* not just to help Christians but to come to the aid of all needy people, the more respect the church will get from outsiders. That said, the churches that made a big impact on me were the ones that knew their "church" was not limited to a building. They made it a priority to spread the *values* of Christianity by serving the *real* needs of people around them. In this case, actions speak louder than preaching.

### *Energy Level and Passion*

The churches I enjoyed the most had a buzz of excitement that was noticeable from the moment I walked in the door. I knew immediately I was in for a good service. It's easy to think this is caused by the look of the church. But I don't agree that bigger and flashier is always better than small and unassuming. I enjoyed the service at Willow Creek Community Church, and they have beautiful buildings and a scenic lake on their campus. I loved Lakewood Church in Houston, which is a former basketball arena with indoor waterfalls. But at the same time, I felt the same thrill at Mars Hill Bible Church in Michigan, whose space is essentially a giant, empty box. A church's high energy level is not produced by meeting in a beautiful building.

The positive feeling I picked up came from other churchgoers. It stands out when you are around people who look forward to coming to church, people who are glad to see one another. That vitality brushed off on me.

At some point, churches need to choose not to invest more money in making their building(s) more aesthetically pleasing or installing better light and sound equipment. The money would be better spent on things that really do generate interest and energy. Bring in a compelling speaker, or sponsor a debate on crucial issues that deeply concern people, or start holding regular question-and-answer sessions. These are things that would bring in those who don't normally attend church. They are also things that would make an outsider realize churches do have something to offer to those who are not already part of the fold. I enjoyed feeling the energy of people who love church, but I'd never experience that if I didn't have a reason to visit a church.

Or think once more about the volunteering idea. Generate energy and excitement by getting more people involved in community service. Use some of the church's money to rent a bus to transport members to a place that needs volunteer help. Do some community service that allows everyone in the church to make a positive impact in the lives of others. Or better yet, donate the money to a charity that helps all people, not just Christians. There are organizations, such as Habitat for Humanity, the Red Cross, Amnesty International, and others, that do work that is consistent with biblical values of helping people who are suffering. If the church seemed more interested in helping needy people, that would be a tremendous statement in its favor in the eyes of the nonreligious. And just as importantly, it would generate interest and involvement among church members.

When people come to church knowing they will have opportunities to help others or, at the very least, to learn something that will change the way they think, they look forward to the service. But if all you have to look forward to is a recitation of Bible verses followed by the church calisthenics of standing up and sitting down, whatever enthusiasm you had at the beginning is quickly drained away. When I was visiting churches, I could predict with great accuracy which churches fit the latter category. All I had to do was look at the disinterested people sitting next to me.

## Dialogue Featuring Opposing Viewpoints

The evangelical world is no stranger to controversy, and it's clear to Christians and non-Christians alike what the standard evangelical stance is on current social, economic, and political issues. While I commend churches that address these issues by bringing in experts on the topic, I'm disappointed that the experts represent only the Christian viewpoint. So here's a suggestion for something churches could start doing—which I observed at only one of the churches I visited: why not sponsor a debate, or at least a discussion, with opposing viewpoints equally represented? If I had seen this sort of thing happening at the churches I visited, I very likely would have gone back to visit them again.

Why is such a dialogue important? Because it shows outsiders that Christians are confident in their beliefs, so much so that they're willing to present their teachings in a setting where the other side of the argument is also presented. If the church has the correct stance on, say, Intelligent Design, then there should be no problem with bringing in a credible evolutionary biologist who can explain the scientific point of view. The church wouldn't lose anything by doing this. In fact, those who attend the program would be able to see firsthand the basis of the "opposition's" viewpoint and how it differs from Christian teachings. The church's representative could explain the Christian view and make it clear how it differs from, in this instance, evolutionary biology. To provide a forum for only the expected evangelical perspective makes it too easy for the church to speak for, or presume to already know, the arguments of the other side. Such an approach makes it seem to outsiders that Christians are afraid to dialogue with someone who represents the opposing viewpoint. Are Christians so weak in their beliefs that such an open forum might cause them to lose their faith?

To gain the respect of more atheists, here is what I would recommend: Bring in someone from the gay community when gay marriage issues arise. Bring in a leader from the Muslim community when you're discussing Islam. Bring in a pacifist when you're considering issues of war, national defense, and militarism.

I have firsthand experience with this. Parkview Christian Church invited me to dialogue with the pastor during a weekend's worth of church services, on questions of faith and doubt. (You can read about this in the next chapter.) The dialogical sermon forced those in the audience to think more deeply about the questions we were raising. Since this was a dialogue between two people who didn't agree on the matter of faith, those in the audience were given a chance to consider arguments from both sides. In a sense, they had to answer for themselves where they stood on the issue of faith. It made questions of faith and doubt much more immediate, and based on their feedback, they *appreciated* the discussion. The dialogue I had with the pastor at Parkview Christian made those in the audience think about these issues in a way a one-sided presentation doesn't.

## Relevant Sermons

Finally, the pastors that made the biggest positive impression on me made sure their message was relevant today. It's useless to explain a Bible story if it doesn't carry with it a *reason* to learn about it. I doubt most people go to church simply to increase their Bible knowledge. They are looking for information that makes a difference in their lives.

The same is true of atheists. We are willing to investigate faith, but we are also looking for something that makes a positive difference. And that's another reason it's essential to be relevant: atheists and most other nonreligious people may not believe many Bible stories are true in a historical sense, and the stories of miracles and other supernatural events also are not accepted as fact. To hear the stories presented without further historical context and no connection to the present is meaningless. So to make an impact, the Bible stories need to be connected to life issues and challenges that are real to people. If the stories can teach me a lesson, they stay with me—even though I'm an atheist.

Researchers have conducted studies that indicate the American public is less committed to church today compared to past generations. For the most part, people in their twenties are not well-versed in the Bible, and many of us don't accept it as a book of divine origin. I'm not suggesting that pastors compromise their beliefs or that they should present the Bible as not being divinely inspired. All I'm suggesting is that to gain a greater hearing among non-Christians, it's crucial that you show that the Bible has something current and relevant to say. The young people who hated going to history class in high school and college are not going to attend church to get another lecture on ancient history. They are looking for something that will help them today.

One thing I always found effective in the churches I visited was that certain pastors followed their retelling of a Bible story with a variety of current applications: Here's how we can be like Joseph at our workplace. Here's how we can emulate Jesus in our relationships. Are you having trouble handling the amount of your schoolwork? Let me point you to a relevant passage in the Bible. This type of preaching and teaching makes the Bible real to those of us who would otherwise disregard it as irrelevant.

And when you're doing this type of preaching, the more examples, the better. Joel Osteen does this every week. But he isn't alone. Many pastors I heard gave interesting examples of how a particular Bible passage became applicable in unexpected situations. They gave personal examples of how they were reminded of certain biblical stories when going through different experiences in their lives. This is the type of preaching that could get through to someone like me.

## Where Churches Are Missing the Mark

Christians stand for ethics and moral living, and I have no problem with that. I stand for those same things. But Christians seem to think they are the *only* people who are concerned about promoting moral living, and the result is an unfortunate us/them view of the world. I can't tell you how many times, when I was sitting in church, the sermon took on an adversarial tone. I found that because I was not a Christian, I was seen as the enemy. Do I have to explain why that made me feel unwelcome?

I don't consider Christians or the church to be the enemy, even though I disagree with Christians in many areas. As I pointed out earlier in this chapter, I admire and support much of the work being done by churches. So why do Christians feel compelled to label everything outside the church as misguided and wrong? If you're trying to reach out to other people, it's not constructive to put up a metaphorical barrier between the two sides.

## A Lack of Sensitivity to Nonreligious People

Since I became an atheist, I've had no problem maintaining my ethics and morals, and I have seen other atheists do the same. In my mind, this counters the argument that someone can't be good without God's help. In fact, I maintain many of the same ethical values I held as a Jain (mental and physical nonviolence, antimaterialism, adhering to the truth), even though years ago I rejected the idea of God.

I share a commitment to Christian ethical and moral *values* without adopting Christian *beliefs*. But many of the churches I visited depicted those who were not Christians as being "lost" or needing to be "saved." Every time I heard this, I felt insulted. What exactly do Christians think they are saving me *from*? A life filled with free inquiry into life's greatest questions? The thought of not having all the answers to these questions? The ability to draw my own conclusions after weighing the evidence? I have felt more satisfied ever since I've considered the notion that no religion or holy book has every answer and every explanation I seek. I'm far from "lost." True, I may not have all the answers, but that's why I appreciate the chance to observe the world around me and search for the answers myself. Just because I'm not a Christian does not mean my life has no meaning.

I didn't become an atheist by accident. I considered the alternatives and weighed the options carefully. I *chose* not to believe in God because atheism made the most sense to me. I would hope pastors and other Christians would recognize that for atheists like me, choosing not to believe was not just a random circumstance but the result of a deliberate process. I would hope that someone who chooses to become a Christian does so after careful investigation, and only after considering the alternatives to belief. I did my own investigation and chose nonbelief. Please don't be angry because I chose the "wrong" answer.

If you want to get through to nonreligious people, you need to first understand where they are coming from. Simply reading a book by former atheist Lee Strobel, such as *The Case for Christ* or *The Case for Faith,* won't cut it. It's true that Strobel converted to Christianity out of atheism, but not all atheists are alike. And beyond that, there are many atheistic responses to the points Strobel makes, which he and other Christian authors fail to address. If you want to understand how an atheist thinks, talk to one who hasn't converted. When I started posting my church critiques on the Off the Map Web site (www.off-the-map.org), an amazing thing happened. Christians and atheists (current, not former) started dialoging. That was months ago, and as of this writing the dialogue continues. Christians and atheists began asking each other questions and listening to each other's answers. I don't know if many of them changed their beliefs, but they certainly learned a lot about what the other side believes and why. It was as if all these Christians had been wanting to talk to bona fide atheists, but didn't know where they could find one. And if you're worried the dialogue got out of hand or became meanspirited, you needn't worry. It is a remarkably civil—though candid—conversation. You will see the same sort of dialogue taking place on my blog, www.friendly atheist.com. I raise questions, and I enjoy the responses from all sides.

I encourage you to seek out atheists or other secular people. They aren't that hard to find. There are atheist groups in all major cities and many smaller ones. There are several national atheist organizations (and leaders) that can refer you to a local organization in your area. A good database for secular groups across the nation can be found at www.atheistalliance.org/directory/list.php. To find secular college organizations, my own group, the Secular Student Alliance, has a listing of affiliates at www.secularstudents.org/node/89. Atheist conventions are held in a variety of locations every year. Attend one. Or find a local atheist and ask the questions you have. I doubt you'd face any antagonism simply for wanting to know where we're coming from. In fact, we'd appreciate the effort you're making to understand us.

If you make an effort to listen to us and get to know us, you'll find out we're not the enemy after all. Do some basic research before you make an assumption about us. If you've read this far, you have a good background in how at least one atheist thinks. We're your fellow human beings who want to live good lives, raise our children to contribute to the good of society, help our neighbors, and be responsible citizens. Yes, we differ on certain social, political, and religious issues. But does that really make us the enemy?

### Too Much Time Devoted to Singing

I have a Christian friend who has heard it said that more churches split over the issue of music than any other issue. I have no idea if that's true, but I can tell you that church music has made a big impression on me—both good and bad. Generally I enjoy the music I hear at churches. However, I'm convinced that a lot of Christians don't care about it. How did I reach that conclusion? Because I saw plenty of people walking in late to the service.

I have the impression that churches begin their services with music to serve as a sort of buffer so that even if churchgoers arrive late, they won't miss the "important" part (that is, the sermon). However, I suspect that as people began to understand that there would be an extended period of music, they started to come in later so they could skip the songs. I can picture the likely progression in my mind. With people coming in later, congregations began singing for longer periods of time...so some of the people came *even later*... so the music lasted longer... See what I'm getting at?

When I visited churches, I actually timed the music portion of the services. At some churches, the praise songs lasted ten minutes, which was fine. But at others, it went on for nearly an hour. That's absurd. A few songs are more than enough to get anyone in the proper mood for church. If the congregation would like to have more time for singing, they could hold a separate event on a weekend.

Speaking of those who walk into church late, I want to know why they do so. Not everyone gets stuck in traffic. If church is so important, there is no reason to walk in late. In fact, if going somewhere to worship God is important, then people should arrive *early.* It seems completely disrespectful to me (and I would think, to the pastors) when people walk into the auditorium five or ten minutes into the service. And what's worse is when parents come in with their children, who learn by example that walking in late is not a big deal. It's just church, right? No need to get there on time. Is that what Christians want to teach their children?

### Not Paying Attention in Church

Some churches have separate services (or Sunday school) for the children at the same time as the main worship service. However, at the churches I visited that did not have a separate event for children, the entire family was in the audience. One would think the adults would be role models, listening to the pastor, maybe even taking notes. Instead, what I saw especially in some of the smaller churches were adults who were obviously bored. They were looking through the program, looking around the room, even looking at their watches. Part of the blame rests on the pastors of these churches (they were among the less-interesting speakers). Regardless, I wonder why these adults come to church in the first place. I would think it's because they believe bringing their children to church is a good thing—or at least something they need to do. But if the parents are bored, you can bet the kids will be bored.

Why am I calling attention to this? For one reason: if you don't like church, then don't go to church. It will just make your kids resent getting out of bed on Sunday. Instead, teach your children at home. You can teach them whatever it is you would hope they'd learn at church. It will be more effective at home, and the children will probably pay closer attention.

## Distracting Behavior During Worship

I understand that different people worship God in different ways, and certainly people should have the freedom to do so. And I realize that at church no one wants to tell somebody else that he or she is worshiping "incorrectly." Still, there were a number of churches, large *and* small, where I was distracted by people who were moving or speaking while the pastor spoke or while the choir was performing. These people seemed oblivious to the things happening onstage. They mumbled to themselves, or they raised their hands and blocked my view of the stage.

I was doing my best to observe all that was going on and to understand what was being said (or sung). So in the interest of those who visit your church, try to get some control over this. I'm not suggesting the ushers run around asking people to kindly shut their mouths and lower their arms. It's a matter of personal responsibility. As an individual, think about how your gestures, movement, and speaking affect those around you.

Look around you. Do you notice people staring at you? Are people quickly looking away when you make eye contact? Are people whispering to the person next to them while they discreetly point at you? Then you're being annoying. Stop it.

## Lack of Opportunities to Ask Questions

The church should be more than a religious club that meets for a couple of hours once a week. I suggested already that there should be more volunteering during the course of the week, but there should also be postsermon programming. It would help alleviate two problems: lack of intimacy at the larger churches and lack of opportunity to ask questions about the points that are raised in the sermon.

At so many of the churches I visited, as soon as the final amen was heard, the majority of people were out the door. Now they could get on with the rest of their lives, it seemed. However, to really have an effective church, there needs to be more than a sermon. Having a program right after the service would be beneficial for those who can't come back during the course of the week. It would also allow pastors of large churches a chance to get to know more of their parishioners. I picture a gathering where people can stay around for food and conversation and where they could ask the pastors questions about the sermon they just heard or other aspects of Christianity that raise questions in their mind.

I left many church services with questions about the sermon. I wanted to know more about certain topics, or I wished I could have certain points clarified. But there was no forum where I could raise these questions. At larger churches, the pastors were rarely around to talk after the sermon. At smaller churches, the only option was to stand in line and monopolize the pastor's time. Wouldn't it be great if immediately after the sermon there was a room I could go to where I could have my questions answered?

I do wonder how many people at the larger churches have had intimate conversations with the pastor. If the pastor could hold a question-and-answer forum after the service, it would allow for a personal connection to be made.

Some churches (New Life Church in Colorado Springs is one example) do, in fact, offer these forums, but they are held on Sunday night or later in the week. That makes it hard for many people to participate. It would be preferable to add an additional hour between services, if your church has multiple Sunday services, for a question-and-answer time. It would be a tremendous benefit to the people who have the greatest need to talk to the pastor.

## Religious Extremism

A number of the churches I visited are influential nationally. They have ministries that reach well beyond their cities. There are also a number of televangelists I haven't met but have heard, so I'm familiar with their views and influence. A lot of these Christian men (they're almost always men) manage to make statements in the name of God that are so ridiculous it makes even many Christians cringe. It certainly provides atheists with a lot of easy ammunition.

*What kinds of statements?* you might wonder. Comments that equate feminism with lesbianism, for example. Or statements that claim atheists like me are the root cause of natural disasters. (God sent a hurricane to partially destroy a city because of the unfaithfulness of its citizens.) You get the idea.

Pastors and Christian leaders who make such statements are not positive role models for anyone. So if Christians by and large agree that such extreme statements are a misrepresentation of God and Christian faith, then why aren't more Christians speaking out *against* the high-profile Christian spokesmen? I can understand that some people may not want to say anything disparaging about powerful, respected people. However, it's easy for atheists to lump all pastors together, as if *every* Christian leader thinks all feminists are lesbians. If you want us to take Christianity seriously, you need to differentiate yourself from those other Christians.

Even at smaller churches, pastors can tell their congregations they are deeply offended by these extreme comments. At least the churchgoers could hear the voice of reason coming from a respected figure.

## Confusing Rituals and Traditions

I know that for many religious people rituals are highly meaningful. I'm not arguing that people should not engage in rituals if they choose to do so. But personally I have a problem with rituals in church for one simple reason: I don't believe everyone present knows why they are performing a certain action.

At some churches I visited I saw people who kneeled before they were supposed to or who said their prayers so quickly it was hard to believe they had put serious thought into them. Were they performing these actions after some deliberation, or were they doing it as a routine matter because they've gone through the motions so many times before? Without knowing why certain actions are performed, the actions are meaningless.

If rituals are done without any understanding of the reasons behind them, then the people need to find out the reasons from their pastors or other knowledgeable believers. No one should perform religious acts mindlessly.

And when I visited churches, even if the members knew why they were going through a ritual, I didn't always know the reason behind it. For example, when worshipers recited certain lines back and forth with the pastor (as I saw at Westminster Presbyterian Church), what purpose did it serve? I already had some knowledge about communion, but if I hadn't had that background, I would have wondered why Christians were drinking wine.

Certainly, I could ask the pastors to explain the rituals. But it would also be helpful to provide a pamphlet that describes all the rituals—and not just the mechanics of each ritual but also the reasons they are done.

I am a naturally curious person, which means I want to know the explanation behind things. One reason I decided to do the eBay auction was because I wanted to find the reason behind religious belief. I know people don't just wake up one morning and choose to believe in God. There are reasons behind it. Likewise, I need to know the reasons behind religious rituals. Rituals should carry clear meaning. If there is no meaning, then why perform them?

It's the same with church traditions. Why structure every church service the same? The best innovations I saw occurred at Via Christus, a house church I visited during my initial research after the eBay auction. A small group of about fifteen people met in the pastor's living room, and the depth of sharing and connection in that small, atypical church far surpassed anything I witnessed at any of the other churches.

At Via Christus, after we listened to a worship song, we spent time going over the lyrics to gain their full meaning. There was a discussion on a few

Bible passages, and Pastor Mike put them in a historical context. I felt like I could interrupt him with questions at any time. Even prayer time, which ordinarily I wouldn't pay much attention to, was made more meaningful because it gave me a chance to reflect on the particular aspects of life we had been discussing. Part of the innovation I'm sure was due to the freedom a house church enjoys, since they operate without the constraints of a large, established church. But the idea that a church would experiment with their approach was refreshing.

It's good to be challenged with novelty in church instead of always sticking to time-honored traditions. Shaking things up makes the experience more meaningful. At a couple of churches I visited, the offering plate or basket was not passed around. Instead, those churches have an area near the doors where contributions can be collected. I like that approach. If someone wanted to make a donation, they could do so anonymously, or at least without calling attention to it. Normally, when the collection plate comes down the row where you are sitting, some people might feel pressure to donate even if they don't really want to or can't afford to make a significant contribution. If they don't make a donation, they feel embarrassed about it. At least that's how I felt. A small innovation, such as allowing people to give an offering at the back of the room, makes a huge difference.

## Intrusive Projection Screens

Now that even small churches have large video screens, it seems like it's impossible to have a church service without them. Okay, I won't complain about projecting the song lyrics on a screen. That's very helpful. But when the pastor is talking, I don't need to be watching a huge, enlarged, video pastor on the screen. If I can't always see the actual speaker, that's all right with me. I prefer that to the intrusion of the television cameras and the dominating video screens. I thought at first that the video screens were for the hearing-impaired, but since I didn't see closed-captioning at the service, I wasn't sure what the reason was other than to show off the church's technology.

While being able to see the pastor might enhance my experience, it's the words that are most important. So tape the sermon if you need to for a television ministry, but roll up the screens for those people present at the service. Force us to just listen. Isn't that why we're in church?

I hope I haven't been too critical of things your church does (or fails to do). The things I singled out for criticism are things that obstruct the message you are trying to communicate. Remember, my critiques are designed to help you see how the Christian message comes across to outsiders.

And now that I've talked about you (if you're a Christian), I'll turn the table and talk about myself. In the next chapter, I'll look at what it would take to cause me to change my thinking about God. What would convince me I'm wrong to deny the existence of God?

Turn the page and I'll tell you.

# What It Would Take to Convert Me

*After Being Exposed to Some of America's Top
Churches, I Still Have Unanswered Questions*

Having completed my churchgoing experiment, the first question that might come to your mind is whether I became a Christian. The answer is no. Did I at least take steps away from atheism? The answer is still no. I'm as much an atheist today as I was before I started attending church.

I did gain a newfound respect for some churches, though, especially those that make a difference by helping all people (Christian or otherwise). These are the churches that *practice* Christianity instead of just preaching it.

Is it possible I might someday become a Christian? I would hesitate to rule out any possibilities, but there is quite a bit that would have to happen before I would decide to believe in God and then consider Christianity. But as I said at the beginning of this book, when it comes to matters of religion, I'm open to the possibilities. I don't believe atheists have all the answers, so I might someday rethink my lack of belief in God. I have thought carefully about what it would take to convince me I'm wrong to deny God, and I explain all of that on pages 172 and 173.

But before I talk more about my own spiritual status (or lack of spiritual status), I want to tell you one last story about a church I visited. This church is unique in that the pastor, Tim Harlow, invited me to take part in the sermon at each of his church's three weekend services. I had visited his church when I was doing my initial research following the eBay auction, and Pastor Tim read my critique of his church posted on the www.off-the-map.org blog. He thanked me for the critique and later invited me to participate in a dialogical sermon with him on the topic of faith and doubt. Because that topic is especially pertinent to this chapter, and because Tim and I had our conversation in front of approximately three thousand people combined in three services, I thought I'd tell that story before I tell you what it would take to convert me to belief in God.

## THE CHURCHGOING ATHEIST GETS A CHANCE TO PREACH

Parkview Christian Church, in the Chicago suburb of Orland Park, has grown rapidly in the past few years. It recently expanded its building to include a state-of-the-art auditorium and space in the lobby where people can have coffee and chat. I became familiar with the church when I visited it soon after the eBay auction. I was surprised that I didn't know about it already, since it is within walking distance from where I lived during high school.

Parkview Christian could also have been my weekend home for a full year. Tim Harlow had bid on me during the eBay auction, all the way to five hundred dollars. He lost to Jim Henderson only in the closing seconds. Had I attended fifty services at his church, which Tim's bid would have paid for, I don't think I would have minded. When I first visited Parkview, I enjoyed listening to Tim speak. He is young and interesting, and though he was talking about the Bible, he made relevant references to pop culture that kept me listening and laughing. This was a guy who knew how to relate to his audience—a guy who drove a Harley onto the stage on Father's Day before giving a sermon on what it means to be a Christian man.

Tim invited me to come back to Parkview for another service. But this time I wasn't just going to watch. I was going to participate. *The Da Vinci Code* movie had just been released, and Tim was doing a series of lectures addressing some of the issues the movie raised: What was the role of women in the church? Could the four Gospels be trusted? What do we really know about Jesus? For the final weekend of the sermon series, Pastor Tim wanted to let the congregation know it was okay to have doubts. And who had more doubts about Christianity than an atheist?

Tim told me that during three sermons, one occurring on a Saturday evening and the two others on Sunday, he and I would ask each other our most burning questions, using a new set of questions for each service. Tim invited his church members to submit questions ahead of time, and during the services the audience was there to listen. In addition to the content of the dialogue we shared, Christians had a chance to observe a calm, rational conversation between a pastor and an atheist. Neither Tim nor I were out for blood. We posed hard questions, and we provided each other with intelligent answers.

Even though this was a church, I felt comfortable accepting the invitation. I wasn't expecting to change many minds over the weekend, but I hoped my questions could be heard by the audience. As I have said before, Christians should not be afraid to contemplate hard questions. If Christianity has the truth, it should stand up under examination. In my dialogue with Tim, I would be raising questions that, years earlier, had driven me away from faith in God. Would it be the same for anyone in this audience, or would they have good answers to the doubts I would reveal?

Before I appeared on stage with Tim, I made it known on my blog that

I'd be doing this. A number of people—both religious and nonreligious—felt this was a really bad idea. Some atheists told me I was stepping into a trap—that this would just be a ploy to try and convert me onstage or lecture against my "immorality." Others said they would love to have an opportunity to speak in front of a large congregation and show them how wrong they were! Those people were missing the point. I wasn't invited to rail against religious belief; I was invited to take part in a dialogue on faith and doubt.

Tim mentioned to me that he noticed many raised eyebrows when he told people at his church what he was planning to do. Some people asked why a church would invite an atheist to speak to people who came to hear the word of God.

Tim and I were confident that good could come out of this experiment. We would not be pointing at each other and saying, "I'm right and you're wrong." The purpose was to discuss our views, explain how we came to them, talk through our differences, and just maybe to concede some points on which we weren't too certain. We felt this would work because we shared a mutual respect for each other.

As the first service began on a Saturday evening, I sat in the audience as Pastor Tim introduced the weekend's theme. "There are some discussions that are just hard to have," he mentioned. Normally, Tim might not have brought up some of the issues that would be raised tonight. If he did, he said, he would have pages of notes ready to refer to. However, he told the audience that if the church wanted to reach out to non-Christians, they needed to be able to dialogue with them, and he wanted to provide a model for doing just that.

As the hour flew by for the first service, we talked about everything from why suffering occurs if there is a loving God, to whether the Bible is inerrant, to the basis for atheists' morals, to Pascal's Wager,[1] to whether good people who follow other religions go to heaven. Different questions along the same lines were raised during the next two services. The audience listened intently as both of us explained our positions and tried to point out, if warranted, where we felt the other was in error. (Some audience members told us later they attended all three services because the discussions were so interesting!) Things were going so well that the dialogues stopped only because our time had expired.[2]

I have stated in previous chapters that I think churches should sponsor open debates, inviting a spokesperson to participate who holds views in opposition to Christian teaching. This is exactly what Pastor Tim did, although we didn't engage in a formal debate. But by his inviting me to take part in a dialogical sermon, the congregation was exposed to an atheist's beliefs along with a Christian response. I wish churches would make this type of dialogue a regular feature of their ministry.

Did Tim and I agree on everything? Of course not. In fact, there were many issues over the course of the weekend where there could be no concessions. For example, I believe in evolution and Tim believes in creationism. When we discussed this issue, it was hard to not let our passions take over; however, we managed to maintain a civil discussion. The point was that our views, while completely opposite at times, were discussed in an open forum. When the churchgoers heard Tim say something they appreciated, they applauded him. When I said something worthwhile, Tim would say I had made a good point. It was that candor that made this discussion different from others I had heard.

Some of Tim's answers were surprising; they didn't match the answers I was expecting from him. For example, he reassured me that not all Christians were of the same mold as the leaders who claim to speak for them. He disagreed with the Christian spokesmen who have blamed natural disasters, such as hurricanes and tsunamis, on God's judgment of wicked people. I asked him to explain what he thought about people who see the Virgin Mary in a grilled-cheese sandwich or Jesus on the side of a highway. I mentioned that it seems to me that people see what they hope to see, not what is really there.

His response: "Explain it to me, man." It was good to hear a Christian pastor agree with me on many of my criticisms, both serious and trivial.

The sessions were not intense the whole time. Before we began each dialogue, Tim reminded his congregation, "Don't clap, okay? This is not a debate. We're coming from two very different places, and so we're going to argue, but we don't want this to be a debate. He's the Friendly Atheist, I'm the Friendly Christian, and you're the Friendly Christian Church. So don't clap for me. And certainly, don't clap for him!" The audience loved Tim's sense of humor, and I appreciated his attempt at leveling the playing field even though we were on his home turf.

After each session, many church members thanked me for sharing my views, even if they disagreed with me. No one said anything negative. Tim said he received the same reactions from the people who spoke to him. This outcome was more positive than I had expected.

When the third service ended, I thought about some of the responses I had given to Tim's questions. They weren't all as clear as I wanted them to be, and I immediately thought of what I should have said instead. Some of Tim's remarks resonated with me, though. They didn't cause me to change my mind, but they helped me understand some of the deeper reasons behind Christian beliefs. I had previously thought certain beliefs were just an easy way out, an excuse for not using your mind. But Pastor Tim explained the thought process behind some of his beliefs, and it helped me better understand his perspective. I also realized that part of the reason Christians don't understand nonreligious people is because we haven't done the best job of explaining ourselves.

For example, Tim stated that he felt science was trying to push God out of the picture. I find this to be a common view among Christians. But I know that isn't really the case. Science deals only with the observable world, so it limits itself to natural explanations. God is supernatural and outside that realm, so science can't make claims about God. (While some atheists would disagree with me on this point, they would agree that science is not *against* God.)

It was hard for me to explain this in a clear way at Parkview Christian Church. I did the best I could under the circumstances, and on some of my responses I could've been better prepared. However, this was an unscripted discussion, and I knew there would be responses I would need to better prepare for in the future.

Another question that was raised was whether my self-characterization as the friendly atheist is the exception rather than the rule among atheists. I would argue without reservation that I represent the vast majority of atheists when I use the adjective *friendly*. But given the image that Christians have of atheists, I realize it would take a long time to convince the Parkview congregation that I'm not an anomaly. But honestly, most atheists don't think we have all the answers, and we're open to having rational discussions with people who think differently from us. We are willing to consider valid arguments that challenge our beliefs.

In all, my dialogue with Tim was beneficial for both sides. If these types of dialogues could take place more often, they would go a long way toward alleviating the anger and misunderstanding that sprouts up so often between the two sides. I would encourage your church to follow Tim's lead. Invite an atheist, an agnostic, or even a religious person who is not a Christian in for a conversation with your pastor. And if you do, please adopt the same ground rules Tim used at Parkview Christian Church.[3]

## Why I Am Still An Atheist

Having reported on my opportunity to "preach" to nearly three thousand Christians, it's time to get personal and reveal some things about myself and the condition of my soul. Since I "sold my soul" on eBay to start this process, how did all the church visits and my interaction with a variety of Christians affect me personally? Where have my months of researching churches and the Christian message left me? Is there anything that would convince me (once again) that there is a God?

## *The Faith Requirement*

Let me begin by talking about the concept of faith. Believing in God requires faith, of course, since God cannot be seen or touched, tasted or smelled or heard. It is because of the faith element that I am an atheist. My sense of logic prevents me from making a leap of faith where none is needed.

For example, some religious people may say children are born only through the hands of God. However, knowledge about the way a sperm and egg operate together gives a logical explanation of the process. I've heard other religious people say evolution might be true, but God had to start the process. While an experiment to create life from scratch has not been replicated in a lab, there are several books that explain how the process could have occurred without God.[4] The same type of theoretical reasoning can be applied to the existence of the universe. My life operates fine without faith. I can still find practical solutions to questions when definite answers are not available.

To convince me I am mistaken in not believing in God, a church would need to appeal to my sense of reason and my insistence on empirical evidence. Every church I went to took so much for granted—without offering reasons for their assertions. It was as if the speakers assumed everyone in the audience was already on board with their lines of thinking, so they didn't bother to back up their statements. But where does that leave someone like me who shows up with a completely different set of assumptions, beliefs, and questions?

While I was listening to sermons, I spent much of my time wondering how the speakers knew the Bible verses they were reading were accurate depictions of historical truth. Of course, I didn't expect the pastors to explain precisely why they believe the Bible is true or how they know God exists. They were speaking mostly to believers who needed no convincing. But perhaps in a question-and-answer forum, which I have recommended before, pastors could entertain the questions people like me would love to ask. These questions are not unusual or atypical—they are the same questions almost all nonreligious people have. They deserve to be taken seriously.

## The Personal Nature of Faith

I realize faith is a very personal thing, because Christians have e-mailed me to say I'm going about this process all wrong. I need to *want* to believe, they say, and I must "open my heart" to God. They tell me I'm thinking too rationally to be convinced. (Of course, I see nothing wrong with thinking rationally. Why shouldn't Christian teachings stand up to reason?)

You won't convince an atheist of God's existence or Jesus' divinity by appealing to his or her emotions. We know better than to believe in something just because it sounds nice. Of course, I would *like* to believe in heaven, but my reason tells me there is no evidence heaven actually exists. The scientific discoveries we all accept without question were not made because the ideas sounded nice. The discoveries were made because the evidence directed scientists to the solution.

Similarly, a Christian must appeal to an atheist's intellect. No church I visited tried to do this. I was never challenged to think more deeply about my questions, or to consider my questions in a new light or from a different vantage point. I wasn't confronted with a new line of thinking that seriously challenged my commitment to empiricism and the scientific method or that attempted to look at science in the context of faith, or vice versa. In short, none of the speakers I heard tried to make a connection between reason and religion. Is it really necessary to let go of reason to have faith?

## The Damage of Faulty Assumptions

If you are a Christian, you agree with me on at least one thing: belief in God is based on faith. But I often wonder if the assumed power of faith can overcome some of the clumsy, ill-advised things that churches do. Do Christians feel that since belief in God requires faith, they don't need to try to make Christianity more welcoming for everyone, especially atheists and agnostics? Does the faith requirement somehow give Christians a free pass to be intolerant, or arrogant, or disinterested in the nonreligious people around them?

Here is an example of how Christians can become more welcoming. They could go to the trouble of getting accurate information about atheism and atheists. What I read about people like me in Christian books and on Christian Web sites is usually inaccurate. Christians need to know who they're talking to if they want to dialogue with nonreligious people. If they don't know what atheism really is, they need to find out by talking to us. If you were going to welcome a guest into your home, and that person came from a different culture, wouldn't you try to learn something about his culture? Atheism is a different culture from Christianity's.

## The Offense of Religious Exclusivity

If Christianity is right in saying God is all-powerful and all-knowing, then God is the ultimate judge of my character and my life. So I don't understand why some Christian groups seek to fulfill that role in our country. Why do Christians think their all-powerful God needs so much help in keeping the atheists in line?

One example that comes to mind is the Boy Scouts, where some young men have been removed from membership because they're atheists. It seems to go against the very teachings of Christ—as much as I know them, anyway. I have read that Jesus went out of his way to spend time with prostitutes and adulterers and tax collectors—those who were "unrighteous" and had been pushed to the fringes of society. He welcomed the company of the same people the religious leaders of that time were criticizing and even shunning. Why would the Boy Scouts not want atheist boys to enjoy the experiences and traditions associated with the group?

A second example is one I've touched on before. Atheists are at a distinct disadvantage in the political realm. A Gallup Poll from 1999 indicated that less than half the country would vote for an otherwise qualified candidate if he or she were an atheist.[5] Again, I find it hard to accept Christianity when atheists are not shown respect simply because of our differing religious views.

I see the same type of religious elitism at work when Christians prefer to do business with other Christians. Some of the churches I visited make Christian business directories available to their members. The implication to me is that non-Christians are not good enough to do business with. Or maybe the assumption is that Christians are necessarily more skilled at plumbing, or auto repair, or practicing law. (I was going to add carpentry to that list, but then I realized you could argue that Christians have an inside track on carpentry.)

Maybe that's not it, though. It might be that these directories are motivated more by a desire to keep the money "within the family." Rather than pay a non-Christian to repair your car, suspecting he might use the profits from his business to buy booze or finance a weekend trip to Vegas, you use a Christian mechanic and hope he devotes his profits to a worthy cause. Is that the reasoning behind it?

The existence of Christian business directories tells me that Christians prefer to associate with other Christians. But how can you demonstrate the advantages of Christian faith if you refuse to associate with people like me? When I observe Christians being religious elitists, it does not make me want to join the club.

This tendency to give preferential treatment to the "in" group goes beyond Christians on a local level choosing not to shop at a store operated by non-Christians. On the national level, most of the Christians who make the headlines are intent on forcing me to conform to conservative political priorities and social restrictions. The spokespeople for these causes too often use the Bible as the *only* basis for their beliefs, ignoring the research done by experts in the subject. If you're a Christian, of course you should use the Bible to guide your life. But when you're trying to convince someone who doesn't believe in the Bible, you must back up your ideas with other sources. I don't see prominent Christians who seek to influence public policy doing that, so it's hard for me to take them seriously.

### The Problem of Preferential Treatment

I have learned that churches are big on mission work, and that Christians enjoy going on mission trips. I have seen positive and negative qualities in roughly equal measure when it comes to mission trips. I've heard church groups talk about having gone to faraway countries, and the accomplishment they seemed to be proudest of was the building of a church in the area they visited. This isn't to say they didn't also bring food, vaccines, and other useful items to the people they were helping, but the newly built church seemed to be what they wanted everyone to know about. My response is that a church building by itself won't help anyone—it's what the people of the church do that makes a difference.

By the same token, many churches boasted about their rate of planting new churches. However, starting a new church is nothing to be proud of— not unless that church is working to improve and serve its community, including all the people who live there. In situations where Christians limit their help to other Christians, the church seems to be more a religious club than a true ministry to others. (I would urge atheist communities to do the same. We may not have nearly the resources churches have, but the more volunteering we do and the more we can use our resources to help those who are disadvantaged, the more atheism will be regarded in a positive light.)

## How to Impress Atheists Like Me

Here is my advice to Christians who want to influence people like me: be open to *reaching out* to people who disagree with you, instead of forcing us to adopt your beliefs in order to win your approval. Why not go ahead and "approve" of me simply because I'm a fellow human? Shouldn't that be enough to earn your respect?

I've read parts of the Bible, a book Christians say they consider to be authoritative. I don't see Jesus insisting that the various "sinners," who were living in his part of ancient Palestine, shape up before he would go to their house for dinner. In this regard, I would argue that atheists are actually following Jesus' example more closely than are a lot of Christians. Atheists are more accepting of those who disagree with them, and atheists don't demand that other people first have to join an atheist club before they will take that person seriously.

Martin Luther King Jr. is said to have observed that eleven o'clock Sunday morning was the most segregated hour in America. Based on the research I did for this book, I would say that still holds true. With very few exceptions, the churches I visited were either black congregations or white ones. (And the pastors were almost always male. And I'm not sure if there is a hidden belief that women don't have the talent or skills necessary to be good pastors, but the female pastors and guest speakers I saw were just as talented as the men. I can't see any reason why women aren't more prominent among the ranks of Christian pastors. Even at the larger churches, there was often the pastor and "the pastor's wife." That's not equal footing.)

You want to reach out to people like me? Then show me the churches where men and women lead on an equal basis, and where I can see a rainbow of people in the crowd instead of a sea of whiteness or, in another neighborhood, a sea of blackness. If you say racial and ethnic segregation in churches comes about because of differing preferences regarding the style of worship, then change the style to one that welcomes everybody. I'd love to see Christian faith leading to openness and equality, respect for people no matter their gender or skin color or language or culture. Think about this: atheist gatherings are often a mixture of everyone in society. The people represent different ethnicities, ages, sexual identities, and races. Does it surprise you that secular people are leading the way in accepting others, no matter their individual differences?

I'm proud that two of the leading national atheist organizations (American Atheists and Atheist Alliance International) are headed by women. Our meetings bring together men and women from different races. You would never see separate sessions held for men and women. We're all equal in atheism, but that doesn't seem to be the case in most churches. I can only wonder why.

## WHY IT WOULD TAKE A MIRACLE

I realize I have wandered from the question that is posed at the beginning of this chapter: is there anything that would convince me I'm wrong about God? I can think of one thing: a miracle. If I witnessed a miracle, that would do it. (This statement might seem out of place given my reliance on logic and reason. Perhaps it is out of place on one level. But remember, I'm just telling you what it would take to convert me.)

When I mention miracles, I'm referring to a *real* miracle, not the type of miracle I heard Christians praying for in prayer meetings. I'll never change my thinking about God based on a "miracle" that helps someone find a better apartment, or the perfect roommate, or a husband. A miracle did not occur when you avoided a car accident. I also don't consider it a miracle if a church gains approval from the city zoning commission to build a parking garage. I'm referring to an obvious, undeniable *miracle*—an occurrence that has no other possible natural explanation.

I've heard reports of amputated limbs growing back and dead people coming back to life. But these things only seem to occur in the absence of video cameras. Why are there no unbiased observers present to verify that the arm really did grow back after a Christian prayed for it to happen? If you want to convince me of a miracle, either I'll have to be there to see it myself or you'll need to provide undeniable proof it actually happened.

## THE NEXT STEP IS FRIENDSHIP

The churches I visited ran the gamut from traditional, to informal, to denominational, to well-established, to emerging. I learned more about the Christian culture than I ever expected to learn when I put up my eBay auction. When I launched this experiment, I wanted to know if I may have missed any sign of God in my path to atheism. I thought that by visiting churches I might see hints of God that I had missed before. I was looking for compelling evidence that would change my thinking.

Now that my experiment is over, I realize I didn't find God, but I saw the incredible power a church can have. I hope that power is used to benefit society instead of hurting it through creating unnecessary divisions between Christians and non-Christians. I hope what I've said will help you, if you are a Christian, to think differently about those who don't share your beliefs.

I have set out on a mission of my own, if you will, to show the world the friendly face of atheism. I would love to meet more friendly Christians. And so would every atheist I know.

Atheists and other religious outsiders are all around you. We work at the same places, live in the same neighborhoods, go to the same movies, and walk our dogs in the same parks. Don't you think it's time we got to know one another?

# Form a Group and Get More from This Book

*by Ron R. Lee*

Hemant Mehta has given you an unprecedented look into the mind of an atheist who immersed himself in the Christian world. Now you can maximize the benefit by talking with other readers about Hemant's observations, questions, and recommendations. Use this discussion guide to explore the points Hemant raised, and gain new insights into ways you can connect more effectively with nonbelievers.

## INTRODUCTION: THE QUESTION OF FAITH

Several years after he became an atheist, Hemant Mehta realized he had never explored what Christianity had to offer before he rejected God. That's how he ended up going to church and exposing himself to the opposing view. To stir interest in his experiment, he launched it with an eBay auction and later decided to use his church visits as a way to help Christians see and hear how they come across to nonbelievers.

1. One of the premises of this book is that Christians who want to communicate the gospel effectively need to listen to the target audience. Now that you have read Hemant's observations about Christians and the church, what did you find most surprising? What did you find most helpful? least helpful?

2. Hemant recalls a story his mother told him, which introduced him to the idea that there are people who don't believe in God. The author concluded that "anyone who believed in a faith differ-ent from that of my family was wrong." Think about stories from your childhood that colored your attitude toward nonbelievers. What were those stories? How did the stories characterize those who don't believe?

3. Hemant describes skeptics as those who don't place their confi-dence in "fables that are meant only to inspire." Were you once a skeptic? How do you differentiate between fact, faith, and fable?

4. As a child, did you accept the literal truthfulness of any fables, such as the Easter bunny, the tooth fairy, or Santa Claus? How did you feel when you later realized these figures were mythical? Did that realization shake your faith in anything else, such as God, your par-ents, or the idea of truth?

5. The author asks, "Why are people unwilling to examine and ques-tion their beliefs?" How would you answer his question?

6. Hemant asserts that he is "a person with questions about faith, an openness to evidence that might contradict my current beliefs, and a curiosity about Christianity and its message." When you read his self-description, what was your reaction? Did you assume that if he

was truly open, he would become a Christian as a result of his churchgoing experiment? Why or why not?

7. The author states that one of the purposes of this book is to "help improve the way churches present the Christian message." Do you agree that an atheist is in a unique position to help Christians present the gospel more effectively? Why or why not?

8. Hemant immersed himself in Christian culture—visiting churches, reading Christian books, talking one-on-one with a variety of Christians. Do you read books by authors who disagree with your religious beliefs? If you do read such books, what have you learned about your own beliefs by reading the ideas of those who disagree with you?

9. The author describes what he considers to be false stereotypes people use to characterize atheists. Write your own list of the characteristics you most commonly associate with atheists. Then compare your list with the author's description of secular people. How do the two lists differ?

## CHAPTER 1: SELLING MY SOUL ON EBAY

In this chapter, Hemant explains why he turned his idea to investigate religion into an eBay auction. But auction aside, the process that led him to immerse himself in the Christian world is enlightening and sometimes surprising.

1. The author explains that after he became an atheist he continued to practice the core teachings of Jainism, his childhood religion. Would you expect an atheist to maintain any religious practices? Why or why not?

2. Hemant writes, "I have noticed that as people grow older, they become much more reluctant to change.... Overall it seems that

people fail to question beliefs that have become safe and comfortable." How might such a tendency prevent nonbelievers from seriously considering the claims of Christ? How might the same tendency prevent Christians from discarding faulty beliefs so they can grow in their understanding of truth?

3.  Hemant reports that Christian friends had cautioned him regarding prominent Christians who are often quoted in the news. His friends maintained that those spokespersons don't necessarily represent the views of most Christians. Who would you recommend that a nonbeliever listen to in order to get an accurate picture of Christian beliefs and values? Why would you recommend that person as a spokesperson?

4.  Hemant's first church experience was attending Mass at a historic Catholic church in Chicago. After observing the rituals, he "was convinced some of [the worshipers] had repeated the same motions their entire lives without really thinking about what they were doing." Do you feel Hemant was assuming too much about the worshipers? Have you ever questioned the value of rituals or the genuineness of people as they are repeating church rituals week after week? Why or why not?

5.  Think about a time when you were a newcomer in a social setting, a religious setting, or a cross-cultural setting. Describe some of the rituals that were unfamiliar to you. Talk about how you felt in that context.

6.  What are the rituals and traditions your church practices that could be confusing to a visitor, even if you are part of a nonliturgical church? How would you explain the meaning behind these practices to an outsider?

7.  When word of his eBay auction got out, Hemant was invited to be a guest on Kirk Cameron's radio program. Before the show was

over, Hemant concluded that Cameron simply wanted to use his story as an excuse to criticize nonbelievers. Reflecting on the radio interview, Hemant asks, "Are comments meant to embarrass a guest and a lack of kindness really accurate representations of Christian compassion?" How do you react to the author's assessment of this Christian radio show? Do you feel an antagonistic approach is ever justified when a Christian is hosting a guest who is a nonbeliever? Why or why not?

8. If you are using this discussion guide with a group, put yourself in Hemant's place as you listen to the two-part radio interview: (www .wayofthemasterradio.com/podcast/2006/02/03/february-03-2006-hour-1 and www.wayofthemasterradio.com/podcast/2006/02/03/february-03-2006-hour-2). Then discuss the feelings you had as you listened to the program's co-hosts comment on Hemant's lack of belief and on nonbelievers in general.

## CHAPTER 2: THE REASONS I LOST MY RELIGION

Hemant was a devout, religious believer before he started questioning the existence of God. In chapter 2, he explains the reasons behind his eventual rejection of faith. His questions and his struggles with belief echo the concerns of many who reject Christianity.

1. "When I chose to reject the idea of God," Hemant writes, "I was motivated in part by facets of my religion that didn't ring true." Have you identified any religious beliefs you have been taught that no longer ring true? If so, what do you do with those teachings?

2. In mentioning that he continues to honor many of the principles of Jainism, the author draws a distinction between religious values and religious beliefs. He supports the values while rejecting the beliefs. Do you agree that the values of a religion can

legitimately be separated from that religion's belief system? Why or why not?

3. When he decided to become an atheist, Hemant risked losing his family's support and his friendships within the larger religious community. In many cultures, a person who chooses to become a Christian risks the same types of losses. Why do you think a teenager would risk such losses in order to reject his faith?

4. After his family moved to Tennessee, Hemant found himself a religious minority in a new school. He states, "Trying to explain my beliefs was a futile, often embarrassing exercise, so I kept my religion to myself." Have you ever felt that way as a Christian? If so, tell about it.

5. The author describes his parents' decision to move back to the Chicago area. The resulting disappointment led Hemant to question God, and he eventually became an atheist. What precipitated your most significant period of questioning God? What was the eventual outcome of your questioning?

6. As he took a hard look at his belief in God, Hemant asked, "Why would God make my life so wonderful in Tennessee, only to take it away so quickly?... I began to think that if God existed, I wouldn't be put in this situation." Have you faced a similar disappointment in life and felt that God had stopped caring for you? Share that story with others in your group. Where did your disappointment lead you?

7. As Hemant researched answers to his questions, he found that atheism resonated with him more than any other view. Does it surprise you that a person who had believed in God all his life would later find the *most convincing* answers in atheism? What would you say to the author to encourage him to continue looking for answers to the God question?

8.  Hemant's advice to Christians who are concerned that their children might abandon the faith is to make sure they know the deeper reasons behind Christian beliefs. He writes, "Don't rely on reasons such as, 'This is what Catholics have always done,' or, 'The Bible says we should do this.'" How do you feel about his advice? Do you agree that Christians—especially teenagers and young adults—need nonbiblical corroboration of the legitimacy of Christian teachings and beliefs?

9.  The author found that "all religions were trying to answer questions they didn't have the answers to. What was so wrong with not knowing?" Would you agree that Christian faith allows for unanswered questions, and that God doesn't give us the answer to every question? If so, do the unanswered questions strengthen your faith or cause you to doubt?

10. Hemant contends that belief in God is learned, not innate. He writes, "I think we're born *without* any knowledge of God and are taught by our parents or other influential people that God exists." Do you believe humans are born with a knowledge of God—or at least with an awareness that God exists? Why or why not?

## Chapter 3: Getting to Know an Atheist

In this chapter, Hemant shows readers what it's like to be an atheist. He also seeks to dispel some false stereotypes about atheists, agnostics, and other nonbelievers.

1.  When you were reading this book, did you consider skipping over chapter 3? If so, did you feel you already knew what atheists think? If you did read chapter 3, were you surprised by any of Hemant's descriptions of atheists and other nonbelievers? What surprised you?

2. One of the author's goals is to help Christians develop a more accurate understanding of atheists and other nonbelievers. Do you agree that Christians are influenced by false stereotypes of those who reject God? If so, give examples of the ways in which those stereotypes come to the surface.

3. The author relates a parable involving the Wind and the Sun, which makes the point that gentle persuasion has more power than coercion. Can you think of situations in which someone tried to pressure you to change your mind, adopt a new belief, or agree with his or her position? How did the approach make you feel? At the time it happened, did you give in to pressure?

4. Hemant reports that when he was a student at a state university, "it seemed that most religious organizations on campus were out to convert me by coercion." When you were in high school or college, were you ever approached by Christians whose evangelistic tactics offended you? If so, what was it about their approach that was offensive?

5. When the author researched student groups on university campuses, he discovered that "The University of Texas at Austin had seventy-four *Christian* groups alone! I couldn't come up with seventy-four reasons that Christians could have for needing separate groups." Why do you think there are so many different Christian groups on the same campus? If you give it serious thought, how many reasons can you come up with for having separate groups of Christians at the same college?

6. Hemant asks, "Wouldn't it be wiser to have one large, united group to achieve a strong Christian presence on campus?" How would you answer that question?

7. The author mentions that the variety of beliefs and the multiple disagreements among Christians mystify him. "I have often asked

Christians why there is such a diversity of thought among them," he writes, "and the response I get often is dismissive: 'That other person isn't practicing the *right kind* of Christianity.' " Have you ever had a similar feeling toward Christians whose beliefs differ from your own? How do you think disunity among Christians comes across to those outside the faith?

8. The author maintains that atheists are discriminated against in the United States. What is your reaction to the story of Herb Silverman—the atheist who initially could not hold office in South Carolina because he did not affirm the existence of "the Supreme Being"?

## Chapter 4: What the Nonreligious Believe

To help overcome inaccurate stereotypes, Hemant feels it's important for Christians to understand what atheists believe. Many might be surprised that atheists have beliefs, because they assume that *belief* implies faith or religious devotion. Not so, says the author.

1. The author identifies the deciding factor in his de-conversion: "I could no longer follow the logic in [Jainism's] most fundamental claims.... But when I reexamined life using the reasoning of atheists, everything started to fall into place." How could atheism resonate with more authenticity than belief in God? If you are using this discussion guide with a group, talk about your responses.

2. Hemant writes, "I appreciate the honesty of an answer that admits, 'We don't know for certain.' " He seems to feel that atheists, more than Christians, are willing to admit they don't have all the answers. Do you agree with his conclusion? Why or why not? Do you feel that most people come to Christianity hoping to get all their questions answered?

3. Here is the author's definition of doubt: "Doubt for me had to do with giving serious consideration to certain religious beliefs and teachings and finding they heightened confusion rather than explaining life as I knew it." Can you understand how religion could actually *create* confusion? How would you respond to Hemant's observation?

4. Here is one example of a Christian teaching that the author can't accept: "There is the belief that murderers who 'accept Jesus' will go to heaven when they die, but someone like Mahatma Gandhi, who used nonviolence to combat India's caste system and to fight for the country's independence, went to hell because he was a Hindu and not a Christian.... How could someone who took another human's life reap greater eternal rewards than a person who dedicated his life to helping others?" How would you answer Hemant's question?

5. The author points out that atheist parents show their children how to "think critically about what society tells them," so they can avoid being deceived by the messages of the culture. Had you ever considered that atheist parents would be concerned about how the culture might corrupt their children? If you are a Christian parent, have you taught your children how to think critically about popular culture so they can differentiate between truth and error in the culture's messages?

6. The author states that when atheists support efforts to remove the phrase *under God* from the Pledge of Allegiance or to remove a nativity scene from public property, they are not motivated by a hatred of religion. "Our real motivation is to respect constitutional guarantees against the governmental establishment of a particular religion," he writes. "If atheists truly sought to remove religion from public life, I would imagine we would fight to change the line

in the Pledge of Allegiance to, 'One nation, under *no* God, indivisible.'" How do you respond to his statement?

7. Hemant refers to "the most fundamental question there is: what is the meaning of life?" Does it surprise you that an atheist agrees that meaning in life is the most fundamental question? Hemant says the atheist answer to that question is that "all people choose the meaning in their lives." How would you respond to that view?

8. The author reports that in every church service he attended, he asked himself, *Does Christian faith answer the big questions of life in a more satisfactory way than nonsupernatural explanations do?* If Hemant asked you that question, how would you answer it?

## CHAPTER 5: THE VIEW FROM A SMALLER PEW

Hemant begins his church critiques with visits to small congregations. Perhaps recalling the closeness he experienced in the religious community of his childhood, he expected to observe a similar closeness among worshipers at small churches. At times, what he encountered was far from what he expected.

1. As you read Hemant's critiques in chapter 5, were you tempted to think that if he only understood what churches are trying to do, he'd be far less critical? If so, do you feel that's a valid objection to some of his critiques?

2. Did the author point out anything about these churches that surprised you, concerned you, or challenged you? If so, which observations elicited such a response—and why?

3. Is there anything in these church critiques that gave you insight or a new perspective on how Christianity comes across to nonbelievers? If so, what were those insights?

4. Did you feel that any of his criticisms were unwarranted? If so, which ones and why?

5. Do you feel any of his comments need to be given careful consideration by the leadership of your church? If so, which comments, and why?

6. Commenting on a pastor in Chicago, the author writes, "Pastor Laura made sure we knew there was a tie between what we heard in church and what we would be challenged by in the coming week outside of church." His implication is that other sermons he heard did not make this connection. Do you agree that such a connection is essential? Why or why not?

7. Pastor Laura asked people in her congregation to write on one side of a piece of paper "what they felt before they were rescued by Christ, and on the other, what they felt like afterward.... I had to wonder: was being down, or lonely, or desperate a prerequisite to finding God?" How would you answer Hemant's question?

8. In DeKalb, Illinois, Hemant visited an Evangelical Free Church. He has some fun with the name of the church: "Maybe it's free of evangelicals? Or does it mean that no one has to give an offering?" Have you ever thought that something Christians take for granted, even something as basic as the name of a church, can be confusing to an outsider?

9. "I noticed something I hadn't expected at a church in a smaller community," Hemant writes. "Most of the families chose to sit by themselves with empty seats surrounding them.... I didn't notice a special bond connecting these families." What would you say to explain the seating choices made by these families? Have you observed this pattern in churches you have attended?

10. At another church, the author notes, "It seemed as if the entire room was full...except for a ten-seat perimeter around where I was sitting. I didn't know if it was because I was sitting with a notebook, writing, or because I was an unfamiliar brown person in a

sea of whiteness, but only when the other areas became crowded did anyone choose a seat closer to me." What's your best theory to explain why the regulars left a buffer of empty seats around this first-time visitor?

11. At a Presbyterian church, the author questions the purpose behind what he calls scripted readings. "If it was meant to energize us about God, you would never have guessed from the dull responses given by the congregation. If it was meant to be a prayer, it gave no evidence of being heartfelt." Does it surprise you that an atheist is troubled by what appears to be a lack of fervor and sincerity in church? How would you respond to the author's observations and questions?

12. The author sums up his criticism of the use of written prayers: "If I wanted to feel close to God, the prayers would have to come from within, tailored to my own struggles, hopes, and gratitude. A scripted prayer took away from all that." How would you respond to his critique?

## Chapter 6: The View from a Midsized Pew

Hemant now switches to midsized churches—or at least churches that have a midsized feel due to the size of the meeting space where the services were held. Among his observations, he identifies a few of the advantages available to churches that have a larger membership.

1. Did the author point out anything about these churches that surprised you, concerned you, or challenged you? If so, which observations elicited such a response—and why?

2. Is there anything in these church critiques that gave you insight or a new perspective on how Christianity comes across to nonbelievers? If so, what were those insights?

3. Did you feel that any of his criticisms were unwarranted? If so, which ones and why?

4. At a church in Colorado, the author was bothered by one line in a song: "One day every tongue will confess You are God" (a paraphrase of Philippians 2:10–11). Do you understand why that lyric troubled him? How would you explain the deeper meaning of the related Bible verse to a nonbeliever?

5. "It seems that pastors in general just assume that everyone in the audience already agrees with them," Hemant writes. "They don't often provide reasons or explanations to back up what they say." Do you agree that pastors should do more to give a larger context and to explain the reasons behind their assertions for the benefit of those visiting the service? Why or why not?

6. Hemant trips over the word *lost* being used to characterize those outside the kingdom of God. "I don't feel lost," he writes. "In fact I've felt found ever since I became an atheist. So I'd like to hear a pastor tell me why he's convinced I am lost." Why do you think such terminology is problematic for nonbelievers? In answer to his question, how would you explain to Hemant why Christians refer to nonbelievers as being lost?

7. At a church in Chicago, the pastor admitted "that even *he* has doubts about God sometimes," Hemant reports. "It was humbling and important to hear that." It's clear that the author was impressed by Pastor Clarence's honesty and transparency. What does that say about the importance of candor and vulnerability when Christians talk with nonbelievers?

8. Pastor Clarence told the story of Doubting Thomas from John 20. Here is how Hemant reflects on this story: "Thomas said he wouldn't believe in the resurrection of Christ unless he saw and

touched Jesus' hands where the nails had been driven in at the crucifixion.... He was asking for the same thing I was looking for: evidence.... Why are atheists so despised for thinking like Thomas
did?" Do you understand Hemant's desire for tangible proof of the
claims of Christianity? How would you answer his question regarding why atheists are criticized for seeking the same thing Thomas
sought from Jesus?

9. At a church in Houston, an announcement was made that a
member of the congregation had died. The author comments,
"The people had prayed that he would get better.... How
was it possible to keep praying for other things when it was
clear that in this instance prayer wasn't working?" How
would you respond to his question regarding unanswered
prayer?

10. The author was frustrated when he heard a speaker say homosexuality was a problem. He continues, "In my view, you are born
either heterosexual or homosexual, so why consider an innate predisposition to be a problem?" How would you respond to his comment? If you stated that Christians oppose homosexual behavior
because the Bible classifies it as sin, and he said he didn't believe
the Bible, what would you say?

11. Hemant continues, "The speaker [at a church] asked us to recite
the following words to begin the process of forgiveness...: 'God,
I love you more than my car, my home, my family...' I couldn't
imagine a person prioritizing God before his wife or their children
or their parents.... Faith might be important, but is it so important
that if we had to choose between family and faith, someone would
tell her family they came in second place?" How would you
respond to the author's question?

## Chapter 7: The View from a Larger Pew

In this chapter, Hemant critiques large churches in three different states. He takes note of a few things that might surprise you, challenge your thinking, or even cause you to raise similar questions.

1.  Is there anything in these critiques that gave you insight or a new perspective on how Christianity comes across to nonbelievers? If so, what were those insights?

2.  Did you think any of the author's criticisms were unwarranted? If so, which ones and why?

3.  Hemant noticed that on Sundays, Second Baptist Church in Houston has as service geared to young adults, and it begins "precisely at 11:11 a.m., a time that holds a superstitious significance for some young people." Were you aware of this superstition? How do you feel about a church starting a service at a time that has superstitious meaning?

4.  The author was curious about one church's twenty-four-hour prayer hotline, so he called the number late at night and got an answering machine. He wasn't experiencing a crisis and he doesn't believe in prayer, but still he was concerned about getting an answering machine and not a human being. How do you feel about a hotline that is manned by a machine? Do you feel Hemant was taking this too seriously? Why or why not?

5.  When the author took note of the worship team at a church in Houston, he realized that "it was apparent that the younger, more attractive singers stood front and center. This was a technique more appropriate for an advertising campaign than a place of worship, I felt." How would you respond to the author's observation?

6.  Hemant read on a church Web site that " 'after meeting at Rolling Meadows High School for seven years, God supernaturally pro-

vided our current main church home…in Rolling Meadows.'
Unless the building suddenly appeared out of nowhere, I figured
there had to be a better word to describe how the congregation
came to occupy its current building." How do you feel about the
word choice on the church Web site? Does the word *supernaturally*
throw you? Can you see how it might confuse someone who is
unfamiliar with church jargon?

7. "One of the main problems I had with the larger churches is the
lack of intimacy between pastor and…what's the word…*pastees?*"
Hemant writes. "Here, though, that problem was eliminated by the
pastor approaching us, *being* one of us." The author is referring to
pastor James MacDonald, who walked down among the people in
the congregation as he was preaching. Does it surprise you that the
connection made by a pastor's simple act was so impressive to a
nonbeliever? What does this say about the need for churches to do
more to establish a connection, and to create a sense of intimacy,
during worship services?

8. At a church in the Chicago suburbs, Hemant was distracted by
frequent quotes from the Bible. "It was as if the pastor felt we
wouldn't believe forgiveness was mentioned in the Bible unless
we heard it repeated, verbatim, from the Bible." How would you
respond to that observation?

9. To some Christians, the author observes, "Preachers such as Joel
Osteen may appear 'watered down' due to the fact that he doesn't
mention Bible verses as frequently as other pastors." Do you agree
that such preachers are watered down? Why or why not?

10. Hemant refers to an anecdote one pastor told that the pastor
claimed was true. Later, the author was unable to find the story
on the Internet, but he located a similar story, which was said to
be a legend.[1] The author comments, "I would expect a pastor to

do more thorough research.... His claim that the story was true without giving a reference caused this pastor to lose credibility in my eyes." Would such an incident cause a pastor to lose credibility in your eyes? Why or why not?

11. The author mentions a prominent pastor who was interviewed in a Richard Dawkins video documentary.[2] "When I watched that video clip," Hemant writes, "I sensed an air of smugness in the way [the pastor] came across." Do you think Christians often come across as smug? If so, what do you think contributes to that impression? What can Christians do to avoid giving the impression that they think they're always right?

12. During a service at a Colorado church, Hemant comments, "For several minutes at a time it was hard to see past the man in front of me, whose arm was raised in praise and blocking my line of vision." Have you ever been distracted in church by the worship habits of other parishioners? If so, what was distracting about the situation? What would you recommend as a solution to such distractions?

13. Hemant feels that Christians are too quick to view outside cultural forces as threats to their faith. He continues, "Evolution is a threat. Gay marriage is a threat. A swear word uttered accidentally on television is a threat.... I don't see how any of these things pose a threat against Christianity. If someone disagrees with you about politics, or social issues, or the matter of origins, isn't that just democracy and free speech in action?" Do you feel that evangelical Christianity is too quick to identify opposing viewpoints as threats? Or would you argue that Christians are too slow to recognize the threats in our culture? Explain.

14. The author asks, "If atheists are willing to debate their beliefs and risk being proven wrong, why aren't Christians willing to subject

their own beliefs—which they hold to be absolute truth—to the same level of scrutiny? Don't they have enough confidence in 'the truth' to believe it will stand against all critics?" How would you respond to this question?

15. The author was impressed by the ethnic diversity of the group that attended a Sunday-night service at The Moody Church in Chicago. Christians know that segregation is common in churches, but have you ever thought that it's a damaging testimony to those outside the church? Explain your answer.

16. Hemant reports that a Chicago pastor commented that "because we couldn't get a handle on Jesus, it was 'proof we didn't invent him!'... The implication was that we wouldn't have purposely created a story that we couldn't fully comprehend." Do you find this to be a persuasive argument for Jesus being God and not merely a prophet or wise teacher? Why or why not?

17. The author says he was offended when a pastor commented that " 'before we're born again, we're spiritually dead.'... It was as if he was saying that if we didn't accept Christ, it was because we hadn't put any serious thought into the question of our existence and purpose, or if we had done so, then we had failed to come up with the right answer." Have you ever thought that nonbelievers might be offended by being characterized with a common Christian phrase such as spiritually dead? Discuss.

## CHAPTER 8: CHURCHES THAT DESERVE SPECIAL MENTION

Hemant visited three megachurches led by well-known pastors. He is generally (but not entirely) complimentary of these churches, and he concludes that one of them is the type of church that would be most likely to cause him to reassess his rejection of God.

1. Did the author point out anything about these megachurches that surprised you, challenged you, or raised concerns? If so, which observations elicited such a response—and why?

2. Is there anything in these critiques that gave you a new perspective on how Christianity comes across to nonbelievers? If so, what were those insights?

3. At Mars Hill Bible Church, one of the pastors pointed out that the local newspaper had reported that the population of those living in poverty in Grand Rapids numbers one in five. "However," Hemant says, "he didn't say anything at that time about what actions the church would take to help remedy the situation, which was disappointing." Do you understand the author's disappointment? Why do you think Hemant keeps returning to the idea that churches should do more to meet the physical needs of people in the community?

4. As Pastor Rob Bell read from John 20, the author reports that Rob "reminded us as we read that we must constantly ask: can we see ourselves in these stories?" Do you see the value of this question for nonbelievers? Why or why not?

5. The author comments, "[Rob Bell's] quirks make him a compelling person to watch. It's the way he talks to everyone as if he were face to face with you in a coffee shop, not as if he's delivering a lecture." This is the second time the author has commented favorably on a pastor who speaks to a huge congregation as if he's carrying on a personal conversation. Why do you feel this stood out to Hemant? How else can speakers convey this sense of intimacy?

6. Hemant acknowledges that his favorite preacher is Joel Osteen. "I can't recall hearing any other pastor talk so much about his or her private life," Hemant writes. "As Joel spoke in front of an arena full

of people, I felt like I *knew* him, at least a little bit." Does it surprise you that a speaker's vulnerability stands out so powerfully to an atheist? Why or why not?

7. Hemant says he left Lakewood Church in Houston knowing that "thousands of people were going to have a better day, and maybe even a better life, after hearing [Osteen] speak.... Everyone is looking for a better life, whether they believe in God or not." The author says addressing this felt need could be a key to attracting nonbelievers to the church. How would you respond to his observations?

8. Hemant suggests that churches would provide a tremendous public service if they hosted debates between a Christian spokesperson and a recognized spokesperson presenting the secular view on the same topic. If churches sponsored such debates, what might they gain and what might they stand to lose?

9. The author concludes, "If any church were to convert me, I felt it would be a place such as Willow Creek [Community Church]. It wasn't a fire-and-brimstone service. It wasn't a worship-God-out-of-fear-of-hell service. It was a place where I could think about the message after I left." What do you think of his assessment? What can churches do to give nonbelievers something to think about after they leave the service?

## CHAPTER 9: WHAT WORKS ON SUNDAY MORNING AND WHAT DOESN'T

After reporting on the churches he visited as he did research for this book, Hemant steps back and provides an overview of the things that impressed him positively—and negatively—about church and Christianity in general.

1. Is there anything in the author's overview that gave you new insight or a new perspective on how Christianity comes across to nonbelievers? If so, what were the insights?

2. Does the author include any critiques of the church in this chapter that you feel are unfair or clearly based on a misunderstanding? How would you clarify those issues for the author if you had the opportunity?

3. Hemant writes, "Too many times I saw churches repeating stereotypes and supporting ideas that seem to go against the very core of what I understood Christianity to stand for. One common attitude justified intolerance rather than emphasizing Christian love." Why do you think nonbelievers often view Christians as being intolerant? Do you feel this impression is conveyed because Christians take an uncompromising stand on scripture, or are Christians actually being intolerant rather than merciful toward others? If you're using this guide with a group, discuss your conclusions.

4. The author is pointed in his criticism of boring preachers, pointing out that regular church attendees seemed to be as bored as he was. Then he praises skilled speakers: "Imagine the best and worst teachers you had in college. The best ones made you want to listen.… They ignited a passion inside you. The best teachers (and the best preachers) connect with something inside you that makes you not just listen, but moves you to *act*." Are you surprised that an atheist who repeatedly appeals to reason and logic is so attracted to communicators who generate passion? How can Christians—in personal interactions and in group settings—communicate in the way he is describing?

5. Hemant recommends that pastors videotape their sermons, but to turn the cameras toward the congregation to record the audi-

ence's response and level of engagement. Is this a good idea? Discuss.

6. In suggesting that churches sponsor debates between Christians and nonbelievers, Hemant argues that it would show outsiders "that Christians are confident in their beliefs, so much so that they're willing to present their teachings in a setting where the other side of the argument is also presented." How do you respond to this rationale? Do you feel the church is overprotective of its beliefs? Do you feel the church is fearful of the persuasiveness of opposing viewpoints? Why or why not?

7. Hemant clearly prefers topical preaching that addresses felt needs. "To gain a greater hearing among non-Christians," he writes, "it's crucial that you show that the Bible has something to say that will help people today." Do you agree that this is necessary to get people to take the Bible seriously? Or should biblical truth be presented on its own merits, regardless of the personal life concerns of those in the audience?

8. The author is sensitive to the frequently expressed attitude among Christians that nonbelievers are "them" and not "us." He writes, "I found that because I was an atheist, I was seen as the enemy." Do you think Christians sometimes ostracize nonbelievers in order to impress on them the error of their nonbelief? Can you give examples of different ways the church projects an adversarial stance rather than a welcoming tone? Do you feel that most Christians are unaware they communicate an exclusive us/them attitude toward nonbelievers?

9. The author feels that Christians fail to seek out nonbelievers to talk to, preferring instead to get their information about nonbelievers from other Christians. Do you agree with his assessment? Why or why not?

10. The author recommends that churches provide regular opportunities for people to ask questions of the pastor. "Wouldn't it be great if immediately after the sermon there was a room I could go to where I could have my questions answered?" he proposes. In his church research, he found only one church that schedules regular question-and-answer sessions. Why do you think more congregations don't provide regular opportunities for interaction, where nonbelievers, spiritual seekers, and believers can raise questions?

## Chapter 10: What It Would Take to Convert Me

It takes guts for an atheist to write a book that helps Christians sharpen their presentation of the gospel—and to end the book by telling believers what would have to happen for him to change his mind about God. But in chapter 10 he is describing how he could be converted.

1. Hemant ended his churchgoing experiment just as much an atheist as when he started. Having read his story, would you say he missed important signs of God's presence? If so, what were those signs? Why do you think he was not persuaded by the things he experienced in church?

2. What would you tell the author that might help guide him toward God, perhaps in a way that he missed during his experiment?

3. Hemant was invited to participate in a dialogical sermon during three services at a Chicago-area church. He reports that some people in the congregation asked the pastor "why a church would invite an atheist to speak to people who came to hear the word of God." Do you agree or disagree with the Christians who hold this view? Why?

4. Hemant feels that pastors need to speak more directly to the concerns and questions of nonbelievers. "Do Christians feel that since

belief in God requires faith, they don't need to try to make Christianity more welcoming for everyone, especially nonbelievers? Does the faith requirement somehow give Christians a free pass to be...disinterested in the nonreligious people around them?" Do you think it's the church's responsibility to focus on the questions of nonbelievers? Why or why not?

5. Hemant says he saw ample evidence that Christians are not interested in befriending or even doing business with non-Christians. "Some of the churches I visited make Christian business directories available to their members," he reports. "The implication to me is that non-Christians are not good enough to do business with." If you are a Christian, do you find that you prefer to do business with other Christians? If so, what motivates you to do so?

6. Hemant continues his line of questioning, "How can you demonstrate the advantages of Christian faith if you refuse to associate with people like me?" How would you answer his question?

7. The author's bottom-line advice to Christians who want to connect with nonbelievers is this: "Be open to *reaching out* to people who disagree with you, instead of forcing us to adopt your beliefs in order to win your approval. Why not go ahead and 'approve' of me simply because I'm a fellow human?" How do you respond to this advice?

8. He offers this additional advice: "You want to reach out to people like me? Then show me the churches where men and women lead on an equal basis, and where I can see a rainbow of people in the crowd instead of a sea of whiteness or, in another neighborhood, a sea of blackness.... I'd love to see Christian faith leading to openness and equality." Do you feel that Hemant is simply parroting the politically correct party line, or is he putting his finger on a valid concern? Discuss.

9. The author finally arrives at the question of what it would take to convince him he is wrong about God. "I can think of one thing," he writes, "a miracle.... I'm referring to an obvious, undeniable *miracle*—an occurrence that has no other possible natural explanation." At this point Hemant is not calling for watertight empirical evidence, but something so miraculous that it would prove that supernatural phenomena are possible. Why do you think he would hold out for a miracle rather than a convincing rational argument?

# Notes

## Introduction

1. The basic idea underlying this story is repeated in many places, and the original source of the story is unknown. The version I relate here is my paraphrase of the anecdote. The famous British preacher Charles Spurgeon referred to a different version of the story in a sermon he preached in 1871. Spurgeon's reference to the story can be found at www.spurgeon.org/sermons/3498.htm (accessed 14 September 2006).
2. I'm serious when I say I'd enjoy hearing from you. You can post your feedback, ideas, suggestions, and responses on my blog, www.friendlyatheist.com.

## Chapter 1

1. Editorial, "Open Your Mind, Shut Your Piehole," *Sidelines,* 30 September 2002, www.mtsusidelines.com/media/storage/paper202/news/2002/09/05/Opinions/Open-Your.Mind.Shut.Your.Piehole-266835.shtml (accessed 17 September 2006).
2. For more information on the man whose forehead was tattooed with a company logo, please see "Heads-Up! SnoreStop Highest Bidder to Place Ad on Andrew Fischer's Forehead for One Month," *Business Wire,* 24 January 2005, www.findarticles.com/p/articles/mi_m0EIN/is_2005_Jan_24/ai_n8706462; or Ina Steiner, "No Snooze for this eBay Auction," 25 January 2005,

www.auctionbytes.com/cab/abn/y05/m01/i25/s07 (accessed 11 October 2006).

3. I made this revision to my initial eBay post just a few days after the auction began.

4. To listen to the two-part radio interview, visit www.wayofthe masterradio.com/podcast/2006/02/03/February-03-2006-hour-1 and www.wayofthemasterradio.com/podcast/2006/02/03/ February-03-2006-hour-2 (accessed 21 October 2006).

## Chapter 2

1. Many experts agree that Jainism is a positive force in the world. In Sam Harris's book *The End of Faith,* the author makes a case that the fundamental adherence of religious beliefs will ruin civilization, since religions advocate the idea that the believer is right and the nonbeliever is an infidel—leading to violence against the opposition. He doesn't spare religious moderates, claiming they help support an environment that makes opposition to religious extremists very difficult. Yet, even Harris concedes: "A rise in Jain fundamentalism would endanger no one. In fact, the uncontrollable spread of Jainism throughout the world would improve our situation immensely." Sam Harris, *The End of Faith* (New York: W. W. Norton, 2005), 148.

2. To add to this mix, between the third and fourth phases of each half cycle, twenty-four *tirthankars* are born, and they enlighten the world about Jainism. As we are in the fifth phase of our half cycle, the twenty-fourth *tirthankar* of this era, Mahavir Swami, has already come and gone. (Historians do place his existence around the years 599–527 BC) For more information, see www.umich .edu/~umjains/jainismsimplified/chapter06.html (accessed 16 November 06).

## Chapter 3

1. Barry A. Kosmin, Egon Mayer, and Ariela Keysar, "The American Religious Identification Survey 2001" (The Graduate Center of the City University of New York), www.gc.cuny.edu/faculty/research_studies/aris.pdf (accessed 29 September 2006). It states that the nonreligious made up 14.1 percent of the American population.

2. The Military Association of Atheists and Freethinkers (www.maaf.info) is a testament to nonbelievers who have served their country in the armed forces.

## Chapter 5

1. The Revised Common Lectionary can be found at http://divinity.library.vanderbilt.edu/lectionary (accessed 4 October 2006).

## Chapter 6

1. For years, the Gallup poll has reported that 42 percent of the U.S. population attends worship services on a typical weekend. However, in recent years, church researchers have taken a more careful look at church attendance statistics. C. Kirk Hadaway and Penny Long Marler, in a 2005 report, concluded that the actual figure is less than 21 percent, or only half the number previously thought to regularly attend religious services. See Hadaway and Marler, "How Many Americans Attend Worship Each Week? An Alternative Approach to Measurement," *Journal for the Scientific Study of Religion* 44, no. 3, September 2005, 307–22, www.ingentaconnect.com/content/bpl/jssr/2005/00000044/00000003/art00009 (accessed 8 January 2007). Church historian Martin Marty of the University of Chicago Divinity School interpolated from Hadaway and Marler's findings that average church attendance in the United

States is just under 163 worshipers, in "Sightings: What's the Count?" The Martin Marty Center, 26 September 2005, http://marty-center.uchicago.edu/sightings/archive_2005/0926.shtml (accessed 8 January 2007). Researcher George Barna has arrived at a much lower number. To see his findings, visit www.barna.org/FlexPage.aspx?Page=BarnaUpdate&BarnaUpdateID=148 (accessed 8 January 2007).

2. Mark 9:22.

3. Mark 9:23.

4. Windsor Village is, in fact, the largest United Methodist Church in North America, with a membership of fourteen thousand. But when you attend a worship service at the church's Heatherbrook location, it has the feel of a much more intimate midsized church.

## Chapter 7

1. The Second Baptist Church Web site says their membership exceeds forty thousand, www.second.org/global/our_campuses.aspx (accessed 4 October 2006).

2. This sentence is quoted on the main page of the church's Web site under "Rolling Meadows (Main) Campus," www.harvestbible.org/Content.aspx?content_id=61 (accessed 1 October 2006).

3. To read this story, see www.baptistpillar.com/bd0512.htm; www.devotions.co.uk/lastsupper.shtml; www.daily-blessings.com/lastsupperp.htm (accessed 11 October 2006).

4. To read about the validity of the Leonardo da Vinci story, see www.snopes.com/glurge/lastsupp.htm (accessed 11 October 2006).

5. The New Life Church Web site says they are a fourteen-thousand-member church, www.newlifechurch.org (accessed 1 October 2006).

6. The Web site of the National Association of Evangelicals says their membership is thirty million, www.nae.net/index.cfm?FUSE ACTION=nae.benefits (accessed 2 October 2006).

7. At the time, Ted Haggard admitted to unspecified "sexual immorality" but denied using drugs, in Paul Asay, "Center Ring of a Media Circus," *Colorado Springs (CO) Gazette,* 9 November 2006, Metro 1, 5, and in Paul Asay and Carol McGraw, "Haggard's Apology Met with Resolve," *Colorado Springs (CO) Gazette,* 6 November 2006, A1, A4.

8. For more information on the documentary *The Root of All Evil?* go to www.channel4.com/culture/microsites/C/can_you_believe_it/ debates/rootofevil.html (accessed 2 October 2006).

## Chapter 8

1. John 20:3–4, 8.

2. Carolyn Kleiner Butler, "Sermon with a Smile," *U.S. News & World Report,* 3 October 2005, www.usnews.com/usnews/culture/ articles/051003/3osteen.htm (accessed 9 October 2006), cites attendance at "more than 30,000." Another article by the same author, however, cites the weekend attendance at Lakewood Church at "some 40,000," Carolyn Kleiner Butler, "Religion in America," *U.S. News & World Report,* 13 September 2005, www.usnews.com/usnews/culture/articles/050913/13religion.htm (accessed 9 October 2006).

3. John N. Vaughan, "50 Most Influential Churches in America," *Church Report,* July 2006, 16–24.

4. To read the story of Joseph, see Genesis chapters 37–45.

5. Matt and Beth Redman, "Blessed Be Your Name" (United Kingdom: ThankYou Music, 2002).

6. For more on the thinking of Francis S. Collins, see his book *The Language of God: A Scientist Presents Evidence for Belief* (New York: Free Press, 2006).

7. Melissa Jenco, "Suburban Churches Reach National List," *Chicago Daily Herald,* 16 July 2006, www.communitychristian.org/dailyed/news_articles/SuburbanChurchnatList2006July16.html (accessed 11 November 2006).

## Chapter 10

1. Pascal's Wager essentially states that given the choice between believing in God and not believing in God, one should choose to believe. If you're right, you will spend eternity in heaven. If you're wrong, no harm is done. All you've "lost" is the minor inconvenience of holding an erroneous belief. However, if you choose *not* to believe and you die and find out you were wrong, you are doomed for eternity. So it's preferable to play the odds and choose to believe, just in case. There are many responses an atheist can give to this, among them that one doesn't know which God to pray to, and that simply saying you believe is not equal to truly believing in the faith.

2. If you would like to listen to our dialogues, look for "A Conversation with the eBay Atheist, Hemant Mehta" at www.parkview church.com/worship/archives.html (accessed 4 October 2006).

3. The practical ground rules we followed were (a) this is a dialogue— a conversation and not a formal debate. So the goal is not to prove that one side is right and the other side is wrong. The goal is greater understanding of what each side believes; (b) even though the dialogue is taking place on the church's "home turf," please refrain from cheering or clapping when the pastor (or whoever represents the Christian viewpoint) makes a point you agree with. This basketball game, and there will not be a winner or a loser;

(c) the Christian speaker would be wise to collect questions before-hand and refrain from allowing the audience to ask questions during the dialogue. This is not because the audience might become unruly, but rather so they can concentrate on listening to the discussion. If they have further questions, perhaps a separate session can be held afterward.

Since no one is keeping score, neither speaker needs to feel overly competitive about the outcome. So make sure the dialogue remains civil and friendly. Show the audience that you really do respect each other. These simple ground rules help to level the playing field for the guest you invite to speak for the other side of the argument. The rules also do a lot to make the dialogue as informative as possible by avoiding a heated debate.

4. If you're interested in reading more on this idea, I would suggest Richard Dawkins, *The Blind Watchmaker* (New York: W. W. Norton, 1986).

5. Frank Newport, "Americans Today Much More Accepting of a Woman, Black, Catholic, or Jew for President: Still Reluctant to Vote for Atheists or Homosexuals," *Gallup Poll*, 29 March 1999, www.galluppoll.com/content/?ci=3979 (accessed 8 October 2006).

## Discussion Guide

1. To read this story, see www.baptistpillar.com/bd0512.htm; www.devotions.co.uk/lastsupper.shtml; and www.daily-blessings .com/lastsupperp.htm (accessed 11 October 2006). To read about the validity of the Leonardo da Vinci story, see www.snopes.com/ glurge/lastsupp.htm (accessed 11 October 2006).

2. For more information on the documentary *The Root of All Evil?* go to www.channel4.com/culture/microsites/C/can_you _believe_it/debates/rootofevil.html (accessed 2 October 2006).

# ACKNOWLEDGMENTS

I wish I could've been in the room when Ron Lee persuaded the decision makers at WaterBrook Press, a publisher that produces books for the Christian market, to offer a contract to an atheist author. Somehow, he was convincing, and WaterBrook took a chance on me. I am grateful to him for that, as well as for his support, guidance, and helping hand throughout the process. This book would not exist without him.

Production editor Laura Wright and copyeditor Melanie Knox also made insightful comments that helped me complete the final drafts.

Others also helped along the way, and while any mistakes are entirely mine, they improved the book significantly. Ana Petrovic and Manisha Sahay read through initial drafts of the manuscript and provided incredible feedback. Anne Kiraly and Rakhee Mitra had words of encouragement whenever I needed them. Keith Matusiak and Chris Prokop always provided constructive criticism and helped me shape my message. Dan Lavoie of the *Daily Southtown* newspaper gave me the first opportunity to voice my thoughts. Fred Edwords helped with a particularly troublesome passage, and the Internet Public Library (www.ipl.org) located a citation that was elusive for so long.

Ashley Gannon accompanied me on one of my church visits and was quick to answer many of my questions. Jacqueline Norton also came on a church trip and was there for me as many of the events in this book took place. The experience wouldn't have been the same without her.

The entire staff and board of the Secular Student Alliance (SSA) encouraged me on this project ever since I first mentioned the idea of the eBay auction. The SSA's executive director, August E. Brunsman IV, has served as a mentor to me for several years. He is an invaluable asset for any organization, and I am lucky to work alongside him.

Duncan Crary of the Institute for Humanist Studies also helped spread word about what I was doing and gave me a practical outline of how to make the most of my experience. I'm still following it.

Wendy Kaminer offered guidance at a point when good advice was hard to come by.

Michael Schaeffer at ICM made several calls on my behalf and later introduced me to agent Kate Lee, who made the entire process run smoothly from start to finish. It was an honor to work with them both.

I owe this whole experience to two people. Jim Henderson gave me the opportunity to take a crash course in American Christianity. I learned more than he could know from our frequent conversations. If you'd like to learn from him, too, I encourage you to read his book *Evangelism Without Additives*. Also, journalist Suzanne Sataline decided to bite on an oddball story and changed my life as a result. It was a pleasure getting to share my first Willow Creek experience with her.

Finally, thank you for reading the words of this atheist. I hope they will spark a discussion in your home, your church, and your community.

A handbook on how to make real connections with nonbelievers, from the winning bidder of Hemant Mehta's eBay soul auction.

Includes 13-Week Study and Discussion Guide

Evangelism WITHOUT ADDITIVES

What if sharing your faith meant just being yourself?

JIM HENDERSON

FOREWORD BY BRIAN MCLAREN

Previously released as a.k.a. "Lost"

Available in bookstores and from online retailers.

WATERBROOK PRESS
www.waterbrookpress.com